They Came to Wake Me

They Came to Wake Me

True Stories of Angels, Healing and Mystical Encounters

Rachel Blacker

Copyright © 2023 by Rachel Blacker

All rights reserved.
No part of this book may be reproduced in any form or by any electronic or mechanical means, including information storage and retrieval systems, without written permission from the author, except for the use of brief quotations in a book review.

First edition June 2023

Cover design by Charlie Blacker

ISBN 978-0-6455191-7-4 (ebook)
ISBN 978-0-6455191-6-7 (paperback)

Published by Soul Connect Publishing
www.rachelblacker.com.au

In loving memory of Noelene

There are more things in heaven and earth, Horatio,
Than are dreamt of in your philosophy.

— William Shakespeare, *Hamlet*

Acknowledgments

for PEOPLE OF EARTH

You are a splendid kaleidoscope of unique creativity, inspiring beyond measure and perfect in each form you take. Thank you for this adventure of life and for contributing to the collective consciousness. Much love.

Contents

Introduction … 13

1. First Contact … 19
2. Thai Prince … 29
3. The Acetic … 35
4. The Ashram … 41
5. Michael … 47
6. Asian Jewels … 55
7. Nine Months of Dreaming … 61
8. An Elfin Village … 67
9. Extraterrestrial Healing … 73
10. Vipassana … 79
11. Molly … 87
12. Phenomenal Cheddar … 93
13. Alacqua … 97
14. The Universe has a Sense of Humour … 103
15. Meeting the Council … 109
16. Ancient Wisdom … 115
17. Suspended In-Between … 123
18. My Angels Besse and Snot … 127
19. Big G … 133
20. What Does it all Mean? … 139

About the Author … 147
Recommended Resources … 149
Also by Rachel Blacker … 151

Introduction

This morning, as I sat, sipping my coffee and overlooking the glassy bay before me, a flood of ethereal memories came drifting into my mind.

On many occasions, I have mused at sharing these with the world. But then, fears of judgement (and perhaps old memories of persecution) have crept in.

And why share these experiences? What is the point, when all we need to awaken spiritually is right here and right now? My spiritual awakening has been a slow one and considering that we awaken in the eternal now, the irony of needing time to awaken is amusingly apparent to me.

Spiritual teachers and authors come in many forms. We each have unique experiences that lend themselves to our perception of the world and our writing. This book is a journey of the relatively unseen world. It is an autobiography of a reality seldom mentioned. It forms a part of my unique spiritual journey and perhaps, you too will have shared some of these experiences.

I share these tales of the unseen at the risk of offering distraction from your spiritual awakening. Therefore, I feel it is important to say this; it is not necessary to actively seek such experiences. Should it be your desire to allow angelic beings into your life, recall past lives, contact other worldly entities or enter the fifth dimension, these things will occur of their own accord. If you crave such experiences, they will elude you.

Begin where you are now. Enter the present moment. Awaken first. Then, should connectedness with the paranormal be required, it will become a part of your experience.

Meditation has been the underpinning factor in my spiritual awakening and it is responsible for prompting awareness of many great mysteries of the universe. It has helped me to be sensitive to my inner knowing through allowing my mind to be still when required. Meditation has also allowed for clear and unadulterated perception. While meditation is not mandatory for awakening, it can be a magnificent tool in contacting the inner depths of your being. I highly recommend introducing a simple meditation routine into your life. There are many free resources available online. I also have some guided meditations and books that assist with meditation available on my website, so I will not outline *how* to meditate in this book. I will, however, state this; meditation is simply setting aside time to be present. As you read through these experiences, I ask that you be present. Being alert and attentive to your body and your breath, will ensure that you remain in the eternal now. As you remain present, you remain open to pure perception, seeing clearly, while remaining free of the shackles of human conditioning.

In the past I have tried to make sense of these events but this robbed me of the gifts they offered. When we reduce the spiritual to a mere intellectual concept, we lose awareness of the power and purity contained therein. I ask that you remain open to the mystery and magic in the words that follow.

When we 'know' only with the intellectual mind, it lessens our ability to receive new knowledge and adapt to an ever-evolving consciousness. In this instance, I am not referring to intuitive knowing, which comes from a deep space within and is simultaneously felt. I am referring to a rigid analytical knowing, that stems from grasping to thoughts in a manner of closed-minded ignorance and is in opposition to your felt oneness with being. It is that voice that tells you 'All pit bulls are aggressive, therefore this one should be put to sleep' when, in fact, that particular pet shows no signs of aggression. When you know something with absolute certainty, it can cloud your perception of present-moment reality.

I will frequently refer to intuitive knowing in this book. Intuitive knowing allows for perception with curious awareness. It's the kind of knowing that arrives in an instant as a 'light bulb' moment and is sometimes referred to as genius or insightfulness. Even then, we do not know with absolute certainty. How can we be so sure in a world that is in a perpetual state of flux? It is for this reason that I steer clear of jumping to conclusions.

It is my hope that this book will bring inspiration. I will share experiences with beings so pure and beautiful, that humans would do good to model their aspirations upon such civilisations. There is much that is lacking in our understanding of the world and what it could be. These experiences will shed a new light upon what is possible in this universe. The impossible is the as yet unimagined. As we open our minds to new possibilities, the ever-changing consciousness and greatest mystery of the universe, we can re-imagine humanity. The experiences I share in this book represent some of what is possible for a new earth.

Introduction

I have a strong sense the beings I have contacted upon my spiritual journey are urging me to put forward their messages. I have been privy to the greatest love imaginable; a love that cannot be fully expressed in words. I am truly blessed to be able to access this connectedness and to have experienced it quietly and alone. It seems it is time to share. Now, they are urging me to connect with you, to share with you these powerful, healing messages. At the heart of these messages is this; you are never alone, you are adored and revered unequivocally, always and forever.

Now, as we move forward, I hope you enjoy these enchanting tales of the mysterious. May you find great healing and inspiration in the pages that follow. As you read, it is my wish for you to sense the love and joy that you are and come to know yourself as that and as the greatest mystery in the universe; the evolving consciousness imbued within all.

Chapter 1

First Contact

I was an exceptionally neurotic young woman. There were many wounds from my childhood that I did not perceive as such. Growing up with trauma was just 'normal.' Drugs were normal. Alcohol was normal. Violence was normal, as was being subservient to an aggressive patriarch. But there was something screaming out inside me, rebelling and raging against it all. It was raging against all the stuff I was told was 'okay.' Those things were not okay. But I was not yet aware of that. I thought there was something wrong with me because, unlike my peers, I didn't know how to be happy. It didn't occur to me to question why. I was an unaware, bumbling mess of reactivity. Although I was uncertain as to *what* was wrong, I knew *something* was wrong. And that was my saving grace.

My body was acting out in a big way. I had been burying my emotions and trying to function in the world. I was working and studying full-time and my body was letting me down. Exhausted and suffering physical pain, I went to several doctors seeking an answer. But no answer was provided except, 'You are perfectly healthy; there is nothing wrong with you.' I'm so incredibly thankful not one of those doctors thought to test for glandular fever, for which they found antibodies several years later. You see, I decided my symptoms were emotional and psycho-spiritual (which in a way, even suffering from glandular fever was due to an energetic misalignment), so I sought relief in the form of a meditation class. That class changed my life.

The first meditation class was unremarkable because I was trying too hard. My mind was actively attempting to conjure the imagery provided by the meditation guide. It was anything but relaxing. I resolved to simply 'let go and let flow' in the next class, without attempting to make anything happen.

When the time came for my second meditation class, that's exactly what I did. I reclined and allowed myself to be perfectly comfortable. I closed my eyes and let myself drift blissfully into the depths of relaxation afforded to me. My attention rested loosely on the voice of the meditation guide, as she gently led us on a journey to a beautiful garden. Joyfully floating, I effortlessly placed one foot after the other, feeling the earth beneath my bare feet, as I made my way to a clearing in the garden. There, in the middle of the clearing, was a large stone pond with a fountain at its centre. I drifted to the pond and sat on the stone edge, gazing at my reflection on the mirrored surface of the water.

Then, to my amazement, upon hearing the words 'But you are not alone,' two figures suddenly appeared beside me in the reflection. To my left was a masculine figure. He was a Caucasian man, with straight brown hair, hanging in a dated 'bowl cut' around his face. And to my right was a feminine figure, glowing in luminescent white light. They told me their names. I heard the name 'Michael' clearly, as if spoken inside my mind. And her name was one I had difficulty remembering, as I had never heard it before. It was a name beginning with 'H,' which I translated to 'Harmony.'

The meditation guide fell silent for a time. It felt like eternity. Michael faded into the background while Harmony became most prominent. She was enormous! I approximate she was ten feet tall. Glowing brilliantly, she had four luminous points of light emanating from her torso, like a four-pointed star. I realised this light was positioned in a way that it almost looked like wings. Yes! That's it! The light could be easily misconstrued as wings! She's what people call an angel!

I found myself with my head in her lap for the longest moment. And for the first time in my life, I felt loved. It was pure; so pure. She knew me; all of me. She could see my heartaches, my challenges, the shadows in my world and she saw me with absolute perfection. She embraced me with an acceptance and adoration that pales in comparison to anything known on this earth. This love, this absolute reverence, *directed at me*, was the most powerful, the most healing experience I had ever known. What had I done to deserve this? Nothing! I had done nothing to deserve it and yet, here I was, being held, cradled in the purest embrace. All of my transgressions were as nothing, dissolved into oblivion, pulverised in the powerful energy of this pure field of light. At first, I cried and cried in what felt like a flood of years of emotions being cleansed from my very being. Vaguely aware of the other meditators, I wailed silently, as snot bubbles and tears streamed down my face. But eventually, I calmed down and remained embraced by Harmony, peacefully enjoying my communion with this magnificent being.

A while later, we were guided to journey back from that exquisite garden, with the assurance we could return at any time. Upon re-emergence, when I attempted to move, every single joint in my body made a cracking sound, even the tiny little joints in my wrists and hands. The aching pains that had plagued me for months were gone in that instant.

The meditation guide went around the room and allowed everyone to speak during the customary debrief. When it was my turn, I told everyone of Michael and Harmony. I spoke of being held by Harmony and the profound experience I'd had, at which point, the meditation guide asked me, 'What did she want you to know?' I thought about it for a moment and responded through uncontrolled sobs of tears, 'That I'm loved!' This simple, yet profound message has appeared repeatedly throughout all of my encounters since.

The meditation guide then shuffled a deck of angel cards and went around the group offering two of them to each of us. I was stunned when I pulled my two cards and looked at them. There they were! Michael and Haniel! It was her! That was the name with 'H' I had been unable to decipher. Haniel! Yes! The image on the card was nearly identical to my vision and I recognised her immediately. The only difference was that her wings were made of feathers instead of white light. Michael also looked the same, with his straight brown hair, only he too had wings and was given the title 'Archangel,' which I suspect is a human convention.

When I returned to my regular life, I felt somehow changed. My mind was opened to new possibilities and to new considerations. Eager to talk about my experience, I made plans to hang out with my best friend and felt my cheeks flush red as I told her what had happened. As I heard the story out loud, I became self-conscious and realised it probably sounded crazy. Consequently, I questioned the reality of what had happened and after several days I came to this conclusion; whether it was 'real' or not is of no consequence. The experience was one of the most profound spiritual moments I've ever had. I was healed. It was positive and beautiful. It stands out to me more than what I had for breakfast that morning (which I can guarantee really did happen). The reality of the experience is irrelevant. There is a lot of evidence in modern psychology to suggest that human perception is subjective. I am not concerned whether these ethereal experiences have a concrete component. It makes no difference to my world to analyse or attempt to prove or measure them. In fact, in over twenty years since this first encounter, I have learned they are best enjoyed as they arise, if they arise and that is all. After this encounter, I remembered an earlier experience that I had written off as being 'just a dream.'

When I was a teenager, I had the worst asthma attack I've ever had. I nearly didn't go to hospital on the first night of the attack on the advice of my dad (he thought I was probably going to be fine). But I knew that if I didn't go to hospital, I would go to sleep that night and never wake up again. I envisioned my dad finding my cold, lifeless body in the morning. It would break his heart. I couldn't do that to him. Between gasps for air, I insisted on going to hospital.

When the emergency department staff rushed to poke and prod me with probes, monitors and cannulas, I knew things were serious. It really was a matter of life and death. They whisked me away to intensive care in a heartbeat. And that is where the real battle began. I was unable to speak or eat; it required too much oxygen to do either. I just had to lay there while my various family members came to visit. I smiled with my eyes to let them know I appreciated them being there. I knew I would be okay now that I was stable and being carefully monitored. I just had to ride it out and hang in there, until my body did its thing.

It was exhausting having my heart-rate elevated at such a dangerous level for so long (a side-effect of the treatment for asthma) and so, after five days, I really wanted to be well again. I cried briefly when I acknowledged this desire and forgot about it.

That night, however, I had a dream. A beautiful, glowing, angel of white light came to me and held me. It felt pure, loving and so very healing. I woke up the next day feeling incredible with barely a sign of the disease that had plagued me in recent days. The nurse who tended to me in the morning was surprised at my rapid recovery and I chirped 'An angel came to me in my dream and healed me!' It was a Friday. I was discharged from intensive care and allowed to return home.

This was my first memory of meeting Haniel, my forever faithful, loving guide. And it turns out I am not the only one in my family to have had her as my guide. Many years ago, my mother told me a tale from her childhood; something I don't believe she has told anyone else. As a young girl she lived in a country town that had frequent electrical storms, where lightning bolts would hit the dry land without any rain falling. During one such storm, my mum was feeling extremely vulnerable and afraid. As she gazed out the window, watching lightning strike the surrounding farmland, a figure appeared. The figure was feminine, about ten feet tall and glowing white, with enormous white wings. My mother felt instantly safe and she knew all was well, even in the midst of the terrifying weather phenomenon. It would seem that Haniel was also there for my mother, reassuring her throughout her short life.

Since these early experiences, the floodgates have opened and the channel of connectedness has been strong. I share these experiences now, bringing a message that is consistent. As humans, we will have challenges in life; all of us, without exception. We each have our unique genetic makeup, our unique circumstances, history and life-situations. Every single individual experience is highly valued by non-physical beings for our contribution to the evolution of consciousness. To come to earth is to accept seemingly insurmountable challenges. Emerging into a physical experience on this planet is the pinnacle of courage and adventure. You are a spiritual warrior and you are at the forefront of creation.

The message is this; you are adored beyond measure. Your unique experience, your contribution to the greatest mystery in the universe, is invaluable. Boldly be all that you are and embrace every ounce of your experience with adoration. You are loved more than you could ever know, you are never alone and you are always 'held' throughout any and all challenges. When you allow yourself to receive, that is the greatest thrill of all, not just for us, as physical beings but also for our non-physical friends. It is pure rapture, the true zest of life and the reason we come into being.

Chapter 2

Thai Prince

My meditation class became the highlight of my week. There was a devoted group of us who attended and we sometimes joked that it was our weekly 'medication.' It was indeed a soothing balm for the soul and necessary for creating a sense of sanity in an increasingly insane world.

One week, the meditation teachers suggested we might do a group past life regression for the following class. While I was open to the idea, I had learned to be without expectation. After a long while of hoping to recreate my experience with Haniel and Michael, I realised the pursuit was futile. Just as no two days in life are ever the same, not a single experience of meditation is the same.

When the evening of the past life regression came, I decided to lay back and relax and if it happened, it happened. At the very least, I would have a nice time basking in the light of presence.

I have no recollection of what was said or how I got to this point but before I knew it, I was standing in the body of a man. I 'knew' much about the life of the man and being in that body felt incredible! His body was balanced and his mind was still, clear and sharp.

The word 'astute' kept repeating during the meditation, as if describing the mind of the man. I didn't know what 'astute' meant at the time and had to look it up in the dictionary later. To my astonishment, it described the man's mind perfectly. I could sense a great deal of vitality and health in the body. There was a notable 'fireball' of energy at the base chakra around my genitals that felt powerful and natural. The man emanated benevolence and gentle strength.

I looked down at my attractive brown feet and noted thick gold anklets on each ankle. As I stood there with my bare feet on the stone floor gazing out of the mountaintop building, it occurred to me that I was in Thailand. I stood there for some time admiring the canopy of the tropical rainforest from above. The orange robes I was wearing indicated that I was a Buddhist monk. This was confusing to me, as I had the sense I was simultaneously a prince, politician and the father of two children; a boy and a girl. I'd previously thought a monk was expected to be a renunciate but this was not the case.

Before long, I was guided to my death scene. I was travelling at night with a convoy. We were headed to an important political meeting via horse and cart. We were ambushed. It was too dark and chaotic to see what happened clearly. All I know is that the horses were spooked while the carts were travelling at speed. The cart I was in rolled over, I was thrown from it and killed instantly. Three things surprised me. One, I was not in the body at the time of death. Knowing my body would not survive the accident, my soul exited early. There was no pain or trauma whatsoever. Two, dying was the most blissful experience I'd had up until that point in my life! It was incredible! I was released into the enraptured oneness from which I had emerged! It was familiar and comforting. I was returning home. And three, I gave no thought to the political condition of my country or to the welfare of my children. I knew that all was well, all was assured and this moment was ordained. My death was final and it was clearly time to move on.

This past life regression helped to explain a seemingly random event that happened on an ordinary evening while I was watching television. It was a few months after I had begun attending my meditation class. As I stared at the screen allowing my mind to drift aimlessly, an impression occurred to me. It was so subtle; it almost escaped my awareness. Thanks to my meditation practice, I was able to 'rewind' my thoughts to access the impression. To my amazement, I saw an image in my mind, like the flash of a memory. In the vision, I was in a rainforest, peacefully contemplating a small Thai Buddha statue. The statue was housed by an alcove, that had been carved into a moss-covered monolith. Sunlight filtered through the dense rainforest canopy, forming beams in the misty air, before landing upon the golden statue. The whole scene was ablaze with golden light and backlit emerald-green foliage. It was extraordinarily beautiful and seemed completely bizarre, that is, until I had the past life regression. I now consider it to be a splendid puzzle piece in a grand mystery.

I was very surprised and delighted that the past life regression was a success for me. In the group debrief, everyone told tales of their past lives and I listened with fascination and wonder. To this day, I draw no conclusions about my past life recollections.

While I don't draw conclusions, I still muse at the apparent lineage of souls. Lineage implies time, yet, in essence, we are timeless and we are one. If we are one, how can I have a specific lineage? If we are timeless, how does my soul appear to have a timeline? Perhaps this is too large a concept for the feeble human mind to grasp. A human mind is a physical instrument, as are words. It becomes difficult to comprehend the metaphysical using physical aids. I have learned to be comfortable with not knowing and allowing these questions to go unanswered. After all, a mystery is no longer a mystery if it is solved. Why be so quick to solve a mystery, when it is exceedingly magical and enticing?

Chapter 3
The Acetic

The thing about past lives is that they are not a part of our present moment reality. While ultimate fulfilment can only occur here and now, we can still learn from the past. It has been an honour and a joy to have flashes of memories showing me what it feels like to be in bodies different to my current body.

If you struggle with your emotional wellbeing in this lifetime, you may benefit from knowing that different bodies have different genetic dispositions, biochemistry and emotional make-ups. In other words, it is easier to be fully awakened in some bodies and more challenging in others. If there is one thing I have learned from experiencing memories of other lifetimes, it's this; no two humans are the same and each experience of life is precious and unique. You will never be who you are right now, ever again. This life is fleeting. I say this not to frighten you but in the hope that it will inspire you to embrace all that you are, even in the midst of every challenge you face. As you embrace all that you are in this moment, you honour your purpose in this lifetime.

My first past life regression opened the floodgates for past memories to drop into my conscious awareness. It also made some earlier recollections make sense. As it happens, I was already in contact with some of my past lives but just didn't understand the significance of the visions I was having.

On an ordinary day, I was walking into my laundry with a basket full of dirty clothes, when I suddenly found myself in the body of a rotund Asian woman. One moment, I'm doing laundry and the next, I'm in the Himalayas, contemplating a vast landscape of snow-capped mountains. I owned nothing aside from my clothes, footwear and heavy furs covering my body. I was a wanderer with no home. My mind was still and my heart chakra was on fire, open, glowing and magnetic. There was a mystical quality to my existence. I understood that I was well-respected and taken into the homes of the villagers, given food and shelter in return for wise counsel. There were times when I was not taken in, which sometimes coincided with severe weather. During these times, I would become so intensely present, it was as though my body would become impervious through being in a state of pure bliss. It was almost as if I would shift into an alternate dimension. The word 'acetic' kept repeating in my mind, as I stood in my laundry absorbing the vision. I did not know what 'acetic' meant at the time and had to look it up in the dictionary afterwards. To my astonishment, it perfectly described the lifetime of this woman. This parallelled my vision of the Thai man, when the word 'astute' repeated in my mind.

This woman will not ever be remembered by history. She was one of the quiet frequency holders of the past and she is forgotten by most. It was easier for her to be fully awakened, given her genetic disposition and the culture in which she was raised. Life was simpler then. I have had many lifetimes during simpler times. It is, however, the Western way of life that has proved to be the most challenging.

The current cultural climate trains the human mind to be constantly busy, distracted and predominantly doing, striving and achieving. To sit and acknowledge ones' discomfort or disease has been discouraged by mainstream culture. Instead, we medicate, rather than delving into the root cause of such difficulties. Please note, that some human bodies, as I have mentioned earlier, have a higher degree of difficulty and may benefit from assistance from modern medications but the medication alone is unlikely to form lasting solutions. Today, many therapies acknowledge the importance of awareness and presence in the transmutation of emotional pain.

It is a tumultuous and unhealthy mind that causes emotional pain. But the mind is not the way to the solution. The body is the way. When we believe every thought we have, especially from a troubled mind, we have an emotional response. This emotional response builds up over time and can feed the thoughts, which in turn, feed the emotion. The way out of this cycle is to simply awaken to the moment. How? Your body is always here and now. Unlike your mind, it cannot be anywhere else in time. There is only this moment. This is your reality. As you breathe consciously, your mind must rest upon the breath, it must return to the body and the now. Here, in this moment, as you become alert to your body and 'come to your senses,' you will find relief from a busy and chaotic mind. You create a sense of spaciousness between 'you' and your thoughts. You observe the thoughts and feelings without adding to the story. They no longer have the power to manipulate or control you. This is when you are liberated from the

The Acetic

thinking mind. There is an aliveness and deep peace that pervades your being. This is a superb lesson from my past lives. Just be here now and now and now. There is only one eternal moment. Allow your mind to be still. Awaken to your moment, here and now.

Chapter 4
The Ashram

After graduating from a science degree in my early twenties, I needed a break from intellectual pursuits and found a job working in a distribution centre for a large supermarket chain. The job was intensely physical and my grey matter was able to chill out for a while. The lifting was extremely heavy. I was one of a group of people recruited at the same time. We went from pasty, chubby and weedy things to intimidating physiques, worthy of a pin-up calendar, in a matter of months. But the sudden muscle bulk had come at the cost of my flexibility. I felt terribly tight and desperately needed relief, which I sought in the form of yoga.

I had already been meditating for a few years and thought yoga was just about the physical body. Of course, I was wrong. Yoga is an entire spiritual philosophy and unbeknownst to me, it was about to take me even deeper on my spiritual journey.

After I had been attending my yoga class for a year or so, my teacher invited me to attend a weekend retreat at the Satyananda Yoga Ashram at Mangrove Mountain. Being a giant nerd with almost no social life, my weekend was conveniently free and I could think of nowhere I would rather be.

Mangrove Mountain and the ashram are absolutely exquisite. There is magic in the land. The sounds of 'aum' reverberate off the natural cliff amphitheatre that hugs the buildings of the retreat. The all-encompassing sounds of bellbirds and cicadas add to the electric excitement, in a celebration of life and form.

I was enthralled with the scent of salt in the air from the tidal inland river, on which the establishment is situated. Drunk on the energy of the place, the words 'high vibration' kept repeating over and over in my mind. The fresh vegetarian food, meditations and people were all a delight. I loved every moment and did not want to return home. This threw my life into disarray.

The ashram provided a stark contrast with the supermarket on the following Sunday night. I had to pick up supplies before returning to work the next morning. The energy was harsh and I was being hit from all angles. The staccato onslaught of shelf-stacking, fluorescent lighting, hollow laughter and checkout beeps was brutal. My sensitivity to energy was heightened. I didn't know how I would ever function in the regular world and I wanted to live at the ashram full-time.

I explored my options and started the process of becoming a student at the ashram. I speak of this as the time I 'almost became a renunciate.' I loathed the material world and everything in it. It all seemed so futile, so pointless. There I was, paying for a car, to go to a job I didn't love, to pay for an apartment I was barely at and none of it brought me satisfaction. I was all set to go with my application, when a very wise swami counselled me into realising I was running away. My purpose was not to be a renunciate or a frequency holder in this lifetime. I was to attempt the greatest challenge of all; the life of a 'householder.'

I threw myself into my yoga and meditation practice. Each morning I awakened early for asana and meditation. Work became an extension of my equanimity practice. Every spare moment, I was meditating, going to retreats at the ashram, attending Maha Mrityunjaya and kirtan. My entire social life revolved around these practices. Most people my age were going to nightclubs on weekends but I preferred drinking chai and chanting. I was transforming my life to become a modern-day monk. The ashram had become my weekend home.

On a weekend retreat, in between yoga classes, I decided to go for a walk in the surrounding bushland to find a place to meditate. As I walked, it was as if the trees were talking to me through the movement of their leaves. It was wind breathing life into the leaves, of course. But how do we know trees don't summon the wind to do their bidding? It felt as if the whole place was alive with energy and celebrating my arrival, like a puppy wagging its tail to greet me.

As I found a perfect place to sit amongst the trees, I decided upon a chakra meditation. This involved observing each chakra point, from my base chakra upwards. When I arrived at the third eye, I saw a solid black ball, like a barren planet. The ball began to crack open and golden light poured from within the cracks, streaming out in all directions. In the space behind my eyes, I could see a deep blue light. The vision was bewildering. I awakened from the meditation in time to hear the call for yoga nidra and made my way to the meditation hall.

After yoga nidra, as I made my way out into the sunshine and back to my dormitory, I had a sudden welling up of emotion. I had barely made it up the stairs to the first balcony when I started crying. I stood at the balcony clinging to the railing, as a storm cloud moved into the valley. It shadowed the sun and rain began falling. As the rain fell, I cried more. The rain became heavier and I wailed. As if spurred on by my howling, the downpour became deafening, giving me permission to just let it all out without a single soul hearing me. My crying ended abruptly and I felt instantly calm. I wiped my tears and the rain stopped, the cloud cleared and the sun returned. I arrived at my dormitory to see my bunk mate in the room. 'What a weird storm that was!' she exclaimed. It was weird indeed.

Had I conjured the storm or did the storm produce in me a healing experience? This is a question I no longer care to answer. We are all interconnected. The earth is an alive and intelligent being. She adores our awareness and appreciation of her. We are literally made of earth components. My body is made of the building blocks that form the physical world. We imbibe the universe and it forms our component parts, held together in a harmonious and mysterious union for only a lifetime. We will disassemble and reassemble. We are transformed but we will never be destroyed; this is the first law of physics. It is foolish to think we are not connected with other life forms on this planet or to view ourselves as isolated and vulnerable fragments.

I present these mystical experiences here not to be solved but to be marvelled at. There is a deep magic imbued within the natural world, of which even the man-made world is an extension. Each item in existence must have within it a life force energy or it simply would not be. The sacred is all around us. It is perceived only when the mind is still. The greatest mysticism available is within you and exists in the eternal now, this magical space out of which all forms are born and to which all forms return. You are one with that.

Chapter 5

Michael

I met Michael for the first time, alongside Haniel, in my second ever guided meditation. Many people refer to him as 'Archangel' Michael but he has never introduced himself this way to me and there is a reason for this. Hierarchy is a human construct. We are as revered and honoured by the angels as they are by us. We are ultimately of the same oneness, in spite of our relative lack of spiritual advancement.

Even at the beginning of a soul's evolutionary journey, we are every bit as valuable as one who has 'attained' divine mastery. Humans use the terms 'old souls' and 'new souls' with either respect or judgement depending on which we are deemed to be. This does not reflect the perspective of non-physical beings, who hold us in the highest of esteem, regardless of whether we are young or old souls. Humans would do good to model this. After having met Michael for the first time, I had very little awareness of any further contact with him in those initial years.

Several years later, I visited the Satyananda ashram. My life was turned upside-down and I morphed into a modern-day Yogi. I was impelled to turn my home into a spiritual sanctuary and wanted to recreate the high-vibration energy I had perceived at the ashram. As I was raising the vibration of my home, I experienced multiple awakenings and emotional releases. Being a sensitive soul born into a harsh environment, there was a dark past in me, which rendered me open to a lot of energies matching that darkness.

One night, sensing I was in danger, I awakened suddenly from a deep slumber. My entire bedroom was icy cold and filled with a highly intelligent malevolence. It felt unearthly; alien and menacing. I'd had some experiences with disembodied beings on the astral planes but this was something else and it was intent on harming me. The fear was so intense, my heart seemed to be thumping out of my chest; it was nearly more than my heart could handle. Then all of a sudden, I 'heard' a silent pulse and saw a flash of electric blue light. My room had been 'zapped' with this blue light and was flooded with warmth in an instant. Calmness immediately washed over me. I knew, without a trace of doubt, that I was safe. My brain, confused by the whole event, wordlessly asked a great big '?' to which I heard the reply 'Michael.' Upon hearing that name, I fell asleep at once.

In the past, I would have *never* gone to sleep immediately after a frightening nightmare. But I just knew I had nothing to fear. The warmth that zapped my room was so powerful, it was impossible to stand in its wake and not be transformed. This event with Michael had me wondering; what if I too, could wield a love so powerful that all malevolence would be transmuted into love?

A short while afterwards, I purchased some Toni Carmine Salerno angel cards. One day, when I was using the cards, I pulled the 'Archangel Michael' card. As I read the description of the card, I was taken by a startling coincidence. The card stated that the Archangel Michael was often associated with an electric blue light and he could be called upon for protection.

It is said that the angels cannot intervene unless we ask them to. This has not been my experience. My angels have intervened, without me having to ask. They will step in if you're in danger and they will offer their help at other times. If you noticed a friend in need, you wouldn't wait for them to ask you for help. You would ask, 'Are you okay?' or 'Is there anything I can do to help?' You would honour their free-will thereafter. Likewise, my angels have frequently asked me, 'Do you wish for my help?' and in most cases I have responded with a resounding 'Yes, please!'

You don't have to ask your angels for help, they will offer it. But you get to choose if you wish to receive it or not. They won't force help upon you; that would be against the laws of free-will. If you do wish for help you may ask. When you do so, it is best to approach it from a state of knowing the help is already received. If you approach your wishes from a sense of lack, you block your ability to receive guidance. The angels stand poised to support you always, no matter what. So rather than saying, 'Please help me with...' it is best to say, 'Thank you for helping me with...' but the exact words don't matter that much. This is just a suggestion to ensure you are in a solution-focused mindset, enabling you to be more receptive.

Michael has shown up in my life at many pivotal moments, without me having to ask and I have always been appreciative of his help; I know he's got my back. Many years ago, before I met my husband, I was swept away in a whirlwind romance. All seemed well, except we had conceived early on in the relationship, which revealed his true colours. The man was terrifying when he found out I was pregnant. It became apparent that I would have to be a single mother. He was not happy with this and insisted on me terminating the pregnancy. He was so desperate to be rid of the baby, that at one point, I feared for my safety.

I was driving up the coast one day and chatting with my best friend about the whole saga, when a sudden pain gripped the lower left side of my abdomen. I 'saw' three electric blue lightning bolts over the area of my left fallopian tube, as three sudden sharp pains simultaneously struck the area. The bleeding began later that day. When I returned to work the following day, the pain and cramping were excruciating. My work colleagues were getting suspicious, as I hobbled to the toilet every twenty minutes or so. I was unable to sleep for three nights and then it all settled down again.

When I went for an ultrasound at six weeks and the baby couldn't be found, I was rushed to hospital with a 'chemical pregnancy.' It is my firm belief that the pregnancy had always been non-viable. Tubal ectopic pregnancies are dangerous and won't ever result in a full-term pregnancy. I suspect I had a tubal ectopic that naturally aborted early on. My life would have been in danger had this not occurred. In hindsight, I am extremely appreciative of this intervention. How could I not feel safe and trust in the flow of life when I have such powerful beings of light at the helm?

In hindsight, I always feel foolish for my lack of trust. Everything has worked out for the best, always. Every single life-situation, every apparent disaster, every frightening detour from my intended path, has always been the right thing. If I look back upon all of my past challenges, there is one lesson that is glaringly obvious; when life appears to be inexorably challenging, it's going to be just fine.

Michael is not only *my* angel. He exists as an omnipresent force of immense love and you too, can call upon him. He is a valiant guardian and protector of the earth and her inhabitants. His love is unwavering and so powerful it can transmute all negativity. I understand the word 'love' has been tainted by thousands of years of misuse. But I have few options in the English language. Let's say that his adoration of this planet and her beings is absolute. He sees all as sacred, without the slightest judgement. Each contribution to the totality of creation is deeply respected and revered. That is the love of which I write. His acceptance of you is pure and without condition. Even if you feel you are the most vile, loathsome wretch of a human, you are adored. When you glimpse this pure, liquid love flowing through your being, you will allow all transgressions to be washed clean.

But you do not need to seek out angelic experiences to know such healing. You have all that you need within

Michael

you right here and right now. When you allow your attention to rest upon this moment, when the mind becomes calm and still, you will sense a subtle aliveness emanating from within. Herein lies deep peace and this is your natural state of being. It is available to you always. The love of which I write is inseparable from who you are. You cannot lose that which you are but the mind can lure your attention away from it. The human mind is noisy and distracting. So, enter this moment. Be still. Become aware of the love that you are.

Chapter 6

Asian Jewels

Although we weren't wealthy, my father worked diligently to make sure I had every opportunity. Being a fisherman was a simple existence but my father had greater ambitions for my future. He used what little money he had to ensure I could wear the finest of garments. Naturally, he believed I was the most beautiful young woman in our small village and hoped the King would notice me on one of his frequent visits to the countryside.

And that is precisely what happened. I was in the right place at the right time and the King was enthralled with my beauty. I was invited to be one of his consorts at the royal palace. My father could barely contain his excitement. But then, he quickly realised he would not see his pride and joy anymore. It was a bitter-sweet moment for him and an aspiration he would come to regret.

The King had a collection of beautiful concubines who were vying for his attention. He was sweet and charming but I sensed that something was awry. I was unable to force myself to warm to him. This led to the revelation of his true colours. There was a thinly-veiled seething pit of darkness within him. In time, I found him to be a vile and repulsive tyrant.

My lack of submission to his will both intrigued and enraged him. He became obsessed with obtaining my love. I was not the most beautiful of the women. I was rather plain by comparison to some of the exceptional jewels of the palace. The King had even managed to acquire a rare albino lady with the whitest of skin, red-hair and soft grey-blue eyes. She and I became good friends.

The King persisted with privileges for me, showering me with gifts and even going so far as to make the concubines tend to me as maids. Some were jealous at first, that is, until they realised my plight. I won their affections and we became very close over time. I was unimpressed by the King's attempts to woo me. He was like a spoiled child throwing a tantrum, desperate to have the one thing that eluded him.

Eventually things became very serious. His obsession grew and he simply could not take my disobedience. The King was accustomed to getting everything the King wanted. But not me. You see, I agreed to a life of service. I was transparent to the light of consciousness, which guided my every moment, as if I were a carriage on a railway track. It would seem I did not have free-will in this particular lifetime but nevertheless, I agreed to this life. I agreed to be the carriage on the railway line and I played my role perfectly.

The King gave me a deadline. I was to agree to marry him or he would end my life. Out of the two choices, the latter was preferable to me and I made this clear. I would not marry the King. He then proposed another, more frightening ultimatum. I was to marry the King in two weeks or he would also end the lives of my maids. My response was simply, 'I do not wish for anyone to be killed nor do I wish to marry the King.'

Had I not been transparent to the light of consciousness, I would have changed the course of history and chosen to save the lives of my maids. But this would have thwarted my purpose.

The day of the execution came. Few were privy to this moment. The King was confident I would change my mind. He waited stubbornly in his palace as the maids and I were ushered into the dungeons below. Dressed in our finest silk garments with elaborate embroidery and expensive dyes, we looked heartbreakingly resplendent.

I watched from afar as my body gracefully followed the hooded executioners down the spiral staircase. The ominous stone walls looked surreal, as they flickered in the glow of the large torches suspended upon them. My maids all quivered as we filed into the small execution room. I remained detached, free of my body, peaceful, as I took note of the room. There were large ornate axes hanging on the walls; a proud tribute to the executioner's craft. In the centre of the room was a raised stone bed; a convenient height for the enormous executioner to perform his task. I watched as my body ceremoniously walked to the stone bed and took its place with the elegance and decorum of a queen. The maids nervously watched on, trembling, looking for any signs that I might waver in my resolve. But they saw no trace of fear as I lay on the cold slab of stone, awaiting my inevitable fate.

The faceless executioner raised a dagger of the finest craftsmanship and drove it deftly through my forehead. I watched as my body convulsed and my eyes rolled back and spasmed. I watched on, unharmed, as I saw bright red blood streaming down my porcelain face, intermingling with my lustrous ebony hair. And I was there; the silent observer, as my maids were laid to waste in a frenzied beheading; large double-bladed axes, swinging in the eerie golden light. All that remained was a warm pile of blood-encrusted fine silk, skin and hair.

The life was now complete and it was time to leave. It would appear as though I did not love the King but alas, this was not so. It was my love for him that led to this life of service. This event showed him that love cannot be bought, manipulated or forced. I was the first person in his life to deny him. He needed to learn that human beings have free will and the right to choose, that not all would bend to his will. And this heinous crime was to be the King's undoing. It was ordained and it was carried out with perfection.

As humans, our understanding of life is limited, to say the least. The memory of this lifetime demonstrates that things are not always as they seem. Even the most bizarre occurrences could be an act of great love. As humans, we do our best to follow a moral code. I have been both victim and perpetrator and neither role is easy to play. If I were to view such lifetimes with heavenly eyes, I would not be so quick to judge another being. The executioners were just doing their jobs. They were respectful despite the horrific task assigned to them. The King was simply playing his part in the evolution of consciousness. I was transparent to the light, a sacrifice to help the King find a lesson he sorely needed. The lifetime was a joy and a tremendous blessing. It was only a short commitment but what an honour to have been invited to play such a role.

Chapter 7
Nine Months of Dreaming

I was devastated when I received news that my closest friend on the planet, my mother, would cease to exist soon. She was given six, maybe nine months to live. A few years earlier, my mum made some significant changes to improve her life situation and apologised profusely for the things I had to endure as a child. I forgave her. At sixteen years of age, she was just a child when she had me. She didn't know any better and I wouldn't be the person I am today, were it not for the bombardment of emotional chaos during my childhood.

My mum was surprised at my distress when she told me her prognosis, as I'd had glimpses of past lives and the continuance of the human soul. She thought I was being too hasty when I wanted to move to her property in Northern New South Wales, so she suggested I should just fly up for a visit instead.

The property is absolutely stunning and very isolated. It overlooks a part of the Great Dividing Range with views of valleys and what Australians call 'mountains,' known elsewhere in the world as 'hills.' Because this was a smoker's household, I opted to sleep outside under the lean-to at the mercy of the leeches and mosquitoes.

At nightfall, the land was just bursting with life! Cicadas, crickets and frogs all competed to be the loudest in a deafening cacophony. The haunting howl of dingoes would occasionally break through the din, adding to the wild and epic ruggedness of this sacred place.

As I drifted in slumber, my mind rested loosely upon the sounds of night, drawing me deeply into an ethereal and timeless journey.

I was everywhere and I was nowhere. I was eternal and simultaneously bound to a point in time and to her, the most beautiful woman and a soul for whom I have the deepest affection. We were entering a covenant together. She was providing a life of service to me. But how would we decide to play it out?

There were two choices. My brother could be born before me and she would remain married to my dad.

Nine Months of Dreaming

The challenges would come in the form of a cold, dull and stifled marriage. But instead, we chose that I would be born first, she would separate from my father early and we would be subject to angry, impassioned outbursts from her various partners. The emotional tapestry was vibrant and rich! Yes! This is the childhood I needed. It would jog my memory perfectly and allow for centuries of wisdom to be downloaded early on in life. It would cause great suffering and require years of healing thereafter. Without the suffering, I would not seek salvation. Yes, indeed, this was the perfect arrangement.

Suspended in nine months of communion with her and with the timelessness, I prepared myself for my arrival. I was eager to come here and connect with her. What a privilege to spend this time together and what an honour to receive her life of service. It must not have been an easy role to play, to struggle so much in life and to believe that you have caused suffering. But it was ordained. We chose it. And so, I forgave her all the more. More accurately, I thanked her, knowing there was nothing to forgive. There was only appreciation for the spiritual growth she gave to me so selflessly.

Being born was a terribly traumatic experience and not just for me. Mortified, my teenage father quietly looked on with his pale face peering over my mother's shoulder. When I emerged, the first thing I remember is desperately gasping for air. I felt so fragile; that life was so fleeting and I had to fight to stay alive. Yes, dying is much more pleasant than the rude shock of emerging into a physical body.

Connected to the oneness, we delight those around us for some time. The mind remains sharp and clear; a receiver for pure thought. Older humans make sounds to describe these pure thoughts but it is not the sound we listen to in these early stages; it is the pure thought to which we pay heed. We understand everything astutely but are not recognised for the intelligence we possess. Eventually we learn to associate the sounds with meanings. They become words. Words are limiting and can never fully express the oneness and the ethereal.

In time, we begin to reduce the sacred and mysterious to mere mental concepts. 'Ah, yes, that's a dolphin. I see those every day. And that's a chair and that's a car. There's that person I had an argument with once; they're a real chore' and on it goes, viewing the world through the filters of a historic past and concepts that exist only in the mind. Moments become dull and lifeless, shadowed by the judgements we impose upon them. Then we spend our time seeking that thing we lost all those years ago. We seek it in material things, status, career success, physical fitness, fantastic spiritual experiences, all the while impelled to move forward. We eventually become disillusioned because nothing of this world really satisfies for long.

The irony is, the very thing that we chase is already here. It didn't go anywhere and we didn't lose it. We just covered it up with the mind, as words and concepts evolved in their complexity. The mind is not an enemy, it has just become way too active and excited with its cleverness. Instead of using the mind, we let it use us; live through us. We are realising now, that living through the veil of the mind is a lacklustre and ultimately dissatisfying existence.

To be able to let the mind idle occasionally, poised and ready for use, enables us to be aware of the eternal now. Colours become more vivid, sounds delight the cells of the body, smells ignite passion, food tantalises the taste buds and life becomes a sensational expression of the sacred and mysterious. Insights and wisdom alight upon the mind, enabling true creative intelligence to emerge.

When you enter the present moment deeply, you return to the oneness; the very space where deep and lasting satisfaction is found. Return to the oneness, then allow thoughts to arise. Return to the oneness, then enjoy your material gain. Return to the oneness, then make the world a better place. Return to the oneness, then allow the expression of all that you are in a celebration of form.

There will never be another like you. Embrace all that you are each and every moment, even if this moment should present shadows of the past. It is through your moments, exactly as they are, that your salvation and satisfaction is found. You have all that you need within you, here and now. The eternal now is all there is. Embrace it as if you have chosen it and allow yourself to be embraced by life. The wonder of creation, even in the most rudimentary of forms, is indeed a marvel. Let life surprise and delight you, as if you are born anew. Awaken in this moment and see life with fresh eyes, for even the ordinary is beyond extraordinary.

Chapter 8

An Elfin Village

After graduating from university, I worked in an office in the city for a while. But I had two lives. I was a professional during business hours and a spiritual seeker every other moment. It would seem my two lives were conflicting with one another. I desperately wanted to be immersed in the natural world, so I quit my office job and moved to the mountains to become an adventure guide.

I was in my element! I would often go camping at night, then pack up my camp early the next morning and head to work.

There was a place I would camp at often, alongside a stream that ran over sandstone and iron ore. I'd had some interesting encounters with wildlife at this place and felt like I was being welcomed by the wilds there.

One day, when I was sunning myself by the stream, a red-bellied black snake came travelling at speed towards me. I sat up when I heard the sound of its body rustling amongst the leaf litter. When it was only a metre away, it stopped still, peering at me with its black eyes, as it tasted the air. The rest of its body didn't appear to receive the message it was time to stop and the remainder of its ample length piled up to its head, coiling itself in a seductive and graceful movement. It stared at me for a moment, as if deciding what to do and then, slowly turned back and left in the opposite direction.

No more than fifteen minutes later, I heard the slithering sound again. This time, it was determined to pass and I was in the way. I sensed no animosity or fear from this animal. In fact, it seemed curious about me and undeterred by my presence. It just wanted to pass. I regret that I army-rolled out of the way. But I was inexperienced with snakes at the time and didn't know red-bellies are not easily frightened, meaning they're quite placid. Most snakes only strike as a last resort, if they feel threatened. I was not threatening to her and she knew it. Would she have slithered right past me and stared at me with curiosity? Could I have shared a unique moment of communion with this beauty? I will never know.

An Elfin Village

As I sat by my camp fire later that night, I sensed I was being watched. I was startled when I peered into the darkness. An elegant fox stood inspecting me from the far reaches of the amber firelight. As her eyes locked with mine, I perceived magic in her. Foxes are introduced to this continent and I had never seen one before. In spite of her designation as feral, I could not help but admire her mystical quality and those intelligent eyes. She slunk off silently into the darkness, leaving a lasting impression on me.

I had not been asleep for long when I could sense a commotion outside my tent. There was a bustling of life that piqued my curiosity. I found myself emerging from my tent into the darkness, only my body was not with me and I could see easily in what had been stifling blackness only hours earlier.

The landscape had been transformed. Previously comprised of unruly shrubs and eucalypts, it was now carefully manicured. It was very tidy with undulating curves following the natural lay of the land. The area looked as though it had been lovingly tended, shaped into a village of sorts. The village was unusual in that there were homes made of living materials, concealed beneath the landscaped gardens. And that is when I saw the inhabitants responsible for the neat little village.

They were slender with pale, almost translucent, skin and were no taller than four feet. Their eyes were large and black and their ears were pointy. I understood that they were nocturnal. I heard the words 'fifth dimension' repeating over and over in my mind. These beings were gentle and sweet. One of the older women knew I was there and she nodded at me approvingly. I watched on as another woman told the children tales of mythical humans, the brutish and frightening giants of the third dimension. The children squealed and laughed, as the animated elder regaled them with tales of these mythical beasts; their shared intent perhaps summoning my invisible presence.

I stayed with the villagers for a while, enjoying their gentle nature. And still, none but the old woman could see me. I listened to their words and I learned of their culture. It was a grave crime to act with violence against nature. Nothing in the natural world was to be destroyed, ever. These people are immersed in a world of enchantment. They are one with the world in which they live and lovingly shape the landscape over time through their intent. The land supports them and tends to their needs in kind.

We are as barbaric monsters to them. We smash, we cut, we explode, we plunder and exploit the natural world. We are loud, clumsy and brash. But they do not judge us. They are wise and know that everything in the great mystery has its place and purpose. Indeed, we do.

There are those who worry about the earth and the challenges she faces because of our barbaric ways. But the earth is not in danger. She knows how to be rid of us. She has been very gracious to host us in spite of our proliferation. What parasite in nature kills its host? This would be a very silly thing to do, considering you depend upon your host for your survival. But that won't be a problem for the earth. Our numbers will simply dwindle. We will perhaps become infertile or something to that effect.

If consciousness wishes to be expressed through humans in continuity, then we will need to have a radical shift towards mass spiritual awakening. We must wake up to this moment. This means to stop periodically, look around, be in the body and really be here. Now, more than ever, it's necessary to be fully anchored in the present moment and lovingly immersed in the world around us. We need to be gentle and kind, which means to release resistance to what is. When we stop resisting life, we allow life to flow *for* us. When we move with the flow of life, we honour our natural world and our earth mother. Intuitive knowing will guide us powerfully and our race will move beyond the danger of extinction.

Chapter 9

Extraterrestrial Healing

As a little girl, I would stare up into the wonder and vastness of space and 'just know' there had to be life on other planets. If observation of nature has taught me anything, it's that there are a myriad of forms repeating over; microcosms representing macrocosms in a seemingly infinite kaleidoscope of creativity. I've since learned that matter, including the human body, is ninety-nine point nine per cent empty space, when viewed at an atomic level. I can't help but draw comparisons with our night sky. While we do see many forms when we gaze up at night, the distances in between those objects are almost incomprehensible.

Humans are yet to definitively decide how many galaxies there are in the known universe but at this point in time, there are an estimated one billion galaxies. In our galaxy alone, it's estimated that there are two-hundred billion stars. Our nearest star, the sun, is about one-hundred and fifty million kilometres from earth. Almost incomprehensible, right?

Common sense tells me it would be ignorant to say with absolute certainty, that 'intelligent' life does not exist on other planets. If you search your house for an odd sock and don't find it, you can't say with absolute certainty it isn't there. You can only confirm your sock isn't in the house, when you find it stuffed in a running shoe in the boot of your car. To say for certain earthlings are the only life forms in the universe, you will need to search the known universe and all alternate universes. Even then, you still won't be satisfied you've searched thoroughly enough.

What I am about to share with you is an experience shared by many earthlings but with a small twist.

It happened one morning, just prior to waking, when I was in that dreamy state, somewhere between slumber and alertness. I don't know when she arrived but I was very appreciative of her assistance. I was in need of healing, as many shadows from the past still plagued me. She knew I was a risk to her. My negative energy could infect her, just like a virus might cause disease in an otherwise healthy individual. She took precautions in the form of a bubble of pure positive energy surrounding her. She hovered above me in her protective forcefield as she went about her work of soothing my emotional wounds.

As I enjoyed this blissful communion, I observed her carefully. She was able to communicate with me wordlessly. I noticed her tiny, vestigial mouth. As I took in this detail, she 'told' me her people no longer needed a mouth to speak, nor did they imbibe the universe through eating. Her pale grey skin made her large black almond-shaped eyes stand out. She had a very large, bulbous head, which she 'explained' gave her the ability to send and receive pure thoughts. Her energy was so gentle and soft, she reminded me of an affectionate feline. I understood that she had travelled from a great distance to spend this time with me. I was honoured and deeply appreciative that such a magnificent being would so generously offer her healing energy.

Upon awakening fully, I was intrigued. She looked just like the stereotypical aliens from many of the abduction accounts and movies, except for one glaring difference; she was not frightening at all. By comparison, I am the frightening one. It occurred to me that she could not only protect herself with a positive forcefield but she could work with the human mind and exploit any existing fears. This would only be used as a last resort, however. I was inspired by her generosity of spirit and her peaceful nature.

Travelling the stupendous distances of our known universe is not a feat that can be achieved through current human technologies that rely on relatively neanderthal means, such as, the use of rocket propulsion. We need a completely different approach if we wish to explore neighbouring civilisations. An appropriate method of transport will only arise in conjunction with great spiritual awakening. Technological advancement alone will not suffice. If science and technology are to enable such explorations, we can only progress by moving into the realms of the metaphysical.

Suffice it to say, I understood that my visitor and her race are vastly more spiritually evolved than humans. At the moment, however, most have a distorted view of her kind. We view her through the same historic veil that is applied to the present reality on earth. We draw comparisons to colonial humans, travelling to unknown lands, conquering and displacing indigenous people in an attempt to gain abundance, power and notoriety. A spiritually advanced society has no need for such ostentations. If an alien is both evolved and intelligent enough to travel to our world, she also knows she simply needs to bide her time, let us kill ourselves through our own stupidity and then peacefully inhabit our planet thereafter.

But she was not here to inhabit our planet. She was here as a part of the oneness, for altruistic and benevolent reasons. She was here to offer herself in service. This was a mutually beneficial healing, for she knows we are of the same source. We are inseparable and as I heal, so too, does she. She was drawn to me in a time of need and it gave her great joy to assist.

In this entire universe, there is nothing to fear except fear itself. Fear incites incapacitation in its passive form and aggression in its active form. Fear is devoid of love and can rob you of the ability to enjoy life. It is a projection into the future of what *might* happen, rather than honouring the unfoldment of each moment. And life will never give you more than you can handle in this moment.

As a living entity, you will one day cease to exist. But fear not. This was always part of the plan. It is true that there will never be another like you on this planet. But who you are is deeper than the form you take and the roles you play in this lifetime. There is a continuity of consciousness that is expressed through you that can never cease to be. You are a representation of an ever-evolving consciousness. You, along with all other life forms, are an aspect of the greatest and most magnificent mystery of all. When you recognise this mystery, that is, the consciousness, in others, you open the door for true communion.

Chapter 10

Vipassana

When I was a young woman, I dated an older man who went missing for a short period of time. Once he'd re-emerged into the world, we caught up and he told me he'd been at a Vipassana meditation centre. He wouldn't tell me much about it; he wanted me to experience it for myself and urged me to attend a ten-day meditation course.

The meditation schedule looked gruelling and I wondered what on earth I had got myself into! And ten days of silence! My mother was doubtful whether I could handle that. Strangely, the silence was the most natural part.

I struggled during the early days of my first Vipassana course. Sitting still for ten hours each day in a cross-legged position was brutal. But I was supposed to be 'equanimous' in spite of the pain. I didn't really understand what that meant. I thought I *was* being equanimous at the time when in fact, my body was tense, which means I was filled with resistance to the reality that was presenting.

About six days in, I was sitting in the usual meditation position, observing pins and needles in my lower legs, ankles and feet, when I became concerned. Would lack of blood flow permanently damage my limbs? As worry took hold, sharp, throbbing pains intensified in the area of my feet and toes. It was almost unbearable, when something miraculous happened. I left my body and the pain vanished. I hovered at the roof of the meditation hall, peering down on myself and the other meditators. The blissful expansion of escapism was delightful but as time went on, the thought arose, 'You know you have to go back in there, right?'

Yes, I had to go back in there. When it was time to leave, I lingered on the roof of the meditation hall, while the other meditators began filing out. I took a deep breath in and sighed, as I accepted the inevitable. It was excruciating. The stabbing pains in my feet had turned to white-hot numbness. All the nerves were screaming out, firing alerts to protect themselves from damage and I had been ignoring them. Two toes from my left foot remained numb for about six months afterwards.

As the course continued, I finally understood what it meant to be equanimous. It was about quieting the mind and not letting it tell you, 'This should not be happening.' Thoughts of resistance, concern and complaint are what caused my pain. During the remaining days, I embraced each moment with reverence and appreciation. I *chose* this. There is no point resisting something that I chose. As I embraced my moments, my moments embraced me. The rest of my meditation course was a blissful marriage of mind and body, receiving insights as to the connection of the two. I could clearly see how my thoughts became feelings, lodged within the body and how those feelings became physical ailments, if left unobserved.

The greatest healing of the physical body comes when we give it our alert attention, without judgement, without allowing the mind to add anything extraneous to it.

My second Vipassana course was equally blissful; ten days of pure stillness, observing the depths of my being.

When I had completed my second course, I thought, 'This is nice but I'd like to be equanimous and blissful out in the tumultuous and chaotic world.' This is a practice that continues to this day.

There are many traditions whereby the body is denied as a means of attaining spiritual ascension. When I first discovered meditation, through my weekly guided visualisation class, my mentors were constantly telling me, 'You're ungrounded. You need to ground yourself.' I would become angry, vehemently denying these accusations. I didn't want them to take my ungroundedness away from me. There was great pain within me and I wished to be free of it. I wanted to escape my body. When I had the opportunity to travel to other realms, it felt good and I craved more of that.

But escaping the body is not a lasting solution. You must return to the body eventually. You can have a multitude of blissful spiritual experiences but until you face what is right here in front of you, there will always be a flipside. You will be at the mercy of the world of polarities; of good and bad, light and dark, birth and death. There's nothing wrong with this, of course, it is simply experiencing a different perspective. It can be quite the roller coaster. Some people pay a lot of money to ride roller coasters, so this form of excitement clearly has its share of appeal.

But should you tire of such emotional upheaval, there is one place where lasting peace is found. It is, in fact, through fully inhabiting your body, that you will find great spiritual 'ascension.' Although, perhaps ascension isn't quite the right word. To describe it as a 'deepening' of spiritual awareness may be more accurate.

Spiritual awakening is no grand achievement. It is your natural state of being that is often covered up by mind chatter. The world provides endless distractions from your true nature. Humans wish to feel good. It is our nature to gravitate towards good-feeling things. People who are on the spiritual path naturally aspire to be kind people and to feel at peace. In most cases, this serves us well. However, if the desire to feel peaceful trumps the need to observe the shadows that lurk beneath the surface, there will be a superficial quality to any happiness that ensues.

I don't advocate for digging up past negative emotions, as anything you need to address from your past will arise, when it needs to, for you to observe now. The key to awakening is to accept your moments as if they are a gift. If you can imagine that everything is arising *for* you and that within each offering lies a great gift, you would be closer to the truth. What if whatever presents to you in each moment *is the key* to your salvation? What would happen if that which appears to be unpleasant at first, is met with curiosity and alert awareness? What if you were able to observe, without drawing conclusions and letting the mind sweep you away in a cascade of rationalisations?

While life will continue to challenge you, it is always working in your favour, even in the midst of apparent turmoil. It is through life's challenges that we awaken. Do not deny what life has to offer you. She is always guiding you, always giving you exactly what you need.

What does your moment give to you right now? Can you embrace this moment with love and reverence? How do you feel in your skin? Can you sense the aliveness that permeates your entire being? What about the breath and the silent, gentle pulse throughout your body? Does any discomfort, agitation or impatience arise? Can you observe that, without trying to be rid of it?

The light of your awareness has great transformative potential. As you allow the mind to be still and rest upon this moment, you allow the light of your awareness to emerge. The body is an excellent anchor to the present moment. When you shine your light upon the body, it benefits enormously. When you shine your light upon the shadows, they too, are transformed into light.

Do not be so quick to escape the body in those painful moments. It is through being here, as a witnessing presence, equanimous and balanced, that you will transmute your shadows. Awakening to this moment is the most natural thing in the world. Whatever this moment brings, embrace it, as if it is the greatest gift ever offered to you. This is how you awaken. Begin in *this* moment. Start where you are, right here and right now.

Chapter 11
Molly

A major benefit of having teenage parents was that seven of my great-grandparents were still alive when I was born. My great-grandfather Frank passed away when I was a baby but I still had the privilege of knowing six of my great-grandparents throughout my childhood. While it was an honour to have known all of them, it is Molly who has found her way into this supernatural tale.

The history books will never mention Molly and as far as I know, she lived a simple life. She raised her children in a small country town in a quaint and tidy house and remained in that house for the majority of her ample days. We would often stay with her when I was a child. I remember her as a bespectacled, purple-haired, slightly hunched lady of cheerful demeanour who was a joy to be around.

I was a young lady when Molly died of old age and I travelled to her hometown for her funeral. It was held at the local Anglican church and there appeared to be hundreds of people present, many of whom were my extended family. What a turnout!

It was yet another dry and sunny day. The local farmers in the family were all chatting about their recent challenges with the drought, as we milled about the entrance of the big old stone building.

I don't remember much of the service except that the inside of the church was exquisite! The archaic stonework showcased tremendous craftsmanship, which conveniently distracted me from the seemingly endless bible passages and 'Amens.'

Soon, it would be time to make our way to the cemetery. After Molly's casket had been carried to the hearse, the church bell began to ring. The haunting clamour of that great bell made my hairs stand on end. How could a single bell echo so loudly? And that is when the storm clouds began to gather at the spire. As the clouds swirled, large rain drops began falling, still centred entirely over the church. Many of the guests had been caught without umbrellas and I donated mine to an elderly couple, never to be seen again.

As we made our way to our cars, the rain fell heavier still. Lightning began unleashing all around us. I gingerly followed the motorcade, peering beyond my frenetic wiper-blades, all the while, marvelling at the white-hot flashes. One of the bolts struck the road and danced like a rebellious child for a moment, before fading away again, leaving its impression etched on my retinas. I had never seen a storm so wild before!

The rain fell relentlessly, as we gathered around the casket for the final part of the ceremony, ready to say goodbye to our beloved Molly. The religious words finally came to a close and the rain eased. To my amazement, while the casket was carefully lowered, the clouds began to break apart. Sunshine re-emerged in its full glory, leaving only the glistening wet earth as evidence of the storm that had just been.

Finally, we were able to mingle again and the storm was the hot topic! My uncle, stating the obvious, said, 'I reckon that was Nan, I do.' We had all been thinking it. Nonetheless, I was very impressed with this spectacular storm and with the magnificent soul of my great-grandmother.

Here she was, a simple, little old lady, living a simple life and she demonstrated great mastery as her final parting gift. It was as though she was showing us, 'I am alive! I am wild! I am free and I am a force to be reckoned with!'

Molly's ecstatic display reminded me that we do not need grand achievements in life, in order to be powerful. The human soul is powerful beyond measure and living a life of humble simplicity is a great contribution to the totality of human consciousness. Today, more than ever, we need those people. They are the quiet, pioneering souls who sow the seeds of blissful harmony. They are the ones who hold the frequency for others to tune into, so that all may one day know the simple joy of being.

Molly reminds us that it isn't necessary to try and be something other than what we are. Are you constantly trying to get somewhere? What if who you are right now is enough?

In a world of discontent, where so many individuals are striving to achieve great material success, in order to alleviate a sense of inadequacy, these people are sorely needed. If you are one such soul, do not underestimate your contribution. Your presence here on earth is invaluable.

If the history books don't remember us, it isn't the end of the world. We do not remember the humans from eighty thousand years ago and this is perfectly natural. Interestingly, those humans didn't go anywhere. They are here, on the earth. Our matter is broken down into its component parts, eventually returning to the cycle of birth and death. The building blocks that formed our ancestors are recycled and become a part of the earth. This is later transformed by plants and other animals into food. We imbibe the world around us and on it goes. We are physically built of our ancestors; we are made of earth. Even in our death, we are contributing to this infinite cycle.

It is extraordinary to think that our ancestors are still here in one way or another. They have gifted us with a magnificent world. This is a gift I wish to honour. I do this simply through appreciation of this moment. That is all. I have Molly to thank for opening my mind to the sovereignty of a humble existence, in its simple perfection.

Chapter 12

Phenomenal Cheddar

My weekly meditation class sustained me throughout my rat race days. I loved walking into that sacred space. There would be angelic music playing, with a collection of stunning crystals sparkling in the soft lighting. It was a joy to mingle with the gentle souls who would attend each week. It felt truly nurturing.

Our meditations would usually follow a simple formula. We would be cleansed and grounded, have a chakra balance and be taken on a journey using guided imagery. Once at our destination, the meditation guide would fall silent. This silence would enable us to connect with a spirit guide or two and receive healing. After a long pause, the meditation guide would begin talking again, offering positive suggestions and then bringing us back out of the meditation.

On the night of the 'phenomenal cheddar,' the silent part of the meditation was most unusual. I was surrounded by beings of white light. I had not encountered them before. They were faceless, glowing orbs, with four large points protruding from their torsos, producing the effect of wings made of light. I recognised one of the beings as having had a life on earth, during which, he was known as Yeshua.

These beings of light gathered around me for a time, channelling white light through the top of my head. It felt like a baptism of sorts. My body felt clear and blissful as waves of perfect harmony washed through me. When I returned to my regular state of consciousness, I had changed. My channel was open and light was flowing abundantly. I was in a state of deep serenity. It would seem I had 'attained' enlightenment. I could not explain it any other way.

I drove home in a bubble of pure bliss and by the time I arrived, I was starving! But there was nothing much to eat in my household except some plain old cheddar cheese. You know, the kind that is labelled 'tasty' as some kind of in-joke amongst cheese manufacturers.

My mind was clear and still, as I sliced some cheddar. I was so intensely present, I felt as if I was an alien who had suddenly landed in the body of an earthling. I observed the action of cutting the cheese with great curiosity. As the knife sliced through the large yellow block, it occurred to me how peculiar the texture was. Stranger still, was the process of eating. What was this, 'eating'? I raised my hand to my mouth and placed the cheese in the opening. I began to chew, all the while noticing what a bizarre act it was. It was sensational! Synapses were firing on my tongue, sending waves of electricity throughout my entire body! The satisfying, creamy texture of the cheddar, as it dissolved and became assimilated into my body, was pure joy. What a peculiar and pleasurable experience!

I had eaten countless times in my life and usually enjoyed my meals but this was something else! I was looking forward to my enlightened state from this night forward. I went to sleep that night, feeling deeply satisfied.

When I woke up the next morning, I felt utterly miserable. I wasn't surprised. I'd had a few 'awakenings' at this point and none of them seemed to last for long. Oh, well. It was back to the wretched rat race as usual.

I learned to accept my awakening experiences when they came. I also knew there was a chance they would not last, based on past patterns. What I did not know, is that enlightenment is the true nature of a human being. After regularly attending the ashram, I had the impression that enlightenment was only for a few select masters. It was made out to be a phenomenal experience and difficult to 'achieve.' But you cannot achieve something you already are. You can obscure it by keeping yourself busy and perpetually giving your attention to a mind that continuously comments, complains and judges.

When you are rendered speechless by great beauty, you sense your true nature. You are the stillness beneath the surface. You are the silence out of which sound emerges. You are the spaciousness that allows all things to be.

Do not seek enlightenment. You are already that. Simply allow the mind to be still when it is not needed. Pause often and allow awareness of your true nature to emerge. And when you are in the awakened state, I highly recommend conscious eating! It's divine!

Chapter 13
Alacqua

When I received news that my mother had no more than nine months to live, I became obsessed by the work of Dr Michael Newton. Dr Newton developed a technique of past life regression that would move clients into realms beyond the death experience and into the 'life' between lives. His books are a fascinating documentation of client accounts, which bare remarkable similarities with one another.

Eager to become a Life Between Lives (LBL) practitioner, I completed the first stage of hypnosis training. I was also curious about my own life between lives and booked some sessions with a practitioner in Byron Bay.

Now, before you get too excited, my LBL session was unsuccessful and I had no recollections beyond the death experience. What I wish to share with you now, is the life of Alacqua.

The LBL practitioner needs a springboard to take you into your life between lives, so a past life regression and death scene is the obvious place to start. In my session, I landed in a most enjoyable past life. I was in the body of a beautiful woman named Alacqua. She was living in the area now known as America, prior to white settlement. Her life was very simple. The small village of Alacqua and her clan, consisted of tepees scattered alongside a river in the midst of a pine forest.

I felt magnetic, walking gracefully with my bare feet on the earth, as my silky black hair cascaded down the small of my back. My radiant, mocha-coloured skin and slim albeit curvy figure, made me very alluring. The old women of my village were eager to marry me off. They were excited about the beautiful offspring I would produce. But this was not to be.

There was only one man for me but he was a traveller. He was tall and handsome and I have fond memories of being embraced by him with my face pressed up against his bare, muscular chest. He stayed in my village for a time but once he left, I didn't see him again. I refused to marry anyone else, much to the disappointment of my elders but I soon found my place within the clan.

I studied medicine with the old ones and it became clear that this was my calling and purpose. My new life path was celebrated and I became a trusted and valued elder. I recall one technique of healing that involved carefully selecting and placing river stones on the back of the patient. This would reinstate the flow of energy along the major energetic centres of the body. It was necessary to use a specific chant to introduce the correct vibration in order to shift any energies that were 'stuck.' Removing blockages using the vibration of the chant, further allowed life force energy to flow.

My life was otherwise unremarkable. But it was simple and pure. It was filled with joy and the deep satisfaction that comes with connectedness; to the oneness, to the clan and to the land. I could feel when my time to leave was approaching and I accepted my transition with grace and ease.

I was initially disappointed that I could not recall the in-between but I trusted this. If I need to remember at any stage, I will. Besides, I have eternity to spend in the in-between, should I wish to do so. After having had these sessions, my obsession with life between lives subsided. I no longer felt the need for the great mystery to be solved and I did not further my hypnosis training. I understood that everything we need is here and now. This one lifetime that I have right now, is an opportunity that will never arise again. There is great value concealed within the individual challenges that every life presents. Each life is unique. That's the whole point. No two lives are ever truly identical, not even that of identical twins.

It is abundantly clear that the creative intelligence, inherent in all things, loves to express itself through form. This life is a celebration of form. I write of mystical encounters and of magical occurrences but the reality is, the world in which we live, exactly as it is, *is* magical! When I think back over this current lifetime and the magic that has occurred with the natural world, I cannot help but be inspired!

I've had conversations with old trees, who have shown me a time-lapse of their view of the sky and told me 'I watched the first ships arrive.' I have had thunderstorms swirl around and within me, as if we were one, as they graced the land with their enormous power. I've had encounters with great marine beasts; sharks, whales, rays, turtles and dolphins, who demonstrate curiosity and display great intelligence in their ancient eyes. The things they must have seen! I have played in bioluminescence in the moonlight, marvelling at the iridescent displays. I have stared for hours into the depths of an amethyst crystal in pure wonderment at how the earth gave birth to such a thing. If I were to continue listing these experiences right now, this book would be thousands of pages long!

I have Alacqua to thank for reminding me to view life as sacred and magical in its apparent 'simplicity.' But of course, the natural world is not simple. It is highly complex and ingenious.

So many spiritually inclined people spend their time desperately craving other worlds and realms, wishing for wonder, connectedness and the return home. But our world is already wonderful and we are already home. Home does not leave us. It is within us; it is who we are. You cannot lose who you are. You do not need to look elsewhere to seek the sacred and the magical. Of all the creations on this planet, you are the most remarkable. You are sacred and magical, as is the world in which you live.

Chapter 14

The Universe has a Sense of Humour

When I was firmly entrenched in my Western way of life, I had an arduous commute to and from the city. Being a modern-day Yogi, I used this as a part of my spiritual practice. I would put relaxing music on, to help ease the tension and I would drive attentively at a comfortable pace. The stop-start traffic was highly unpredictable and it was safe to leave a gap of at least a car space, much to the distaste of the other commuters.

The culture was to tailgate but this required adrenaline-pumping focus and a few instant coffees. I still remember the face of one lady clearly, as she sped around me in the adjacent lane, snarling at me through her window because I was not tailgating the person in front of me. I was a young woman at the time and it was odd to see one of my elders behaving like a toddler throwing a tantrum. I simply looked at her with curious detachment, as her contorted face mouthed profanities.

I was very sensitive to the energies around me and the Western Sydney commute provided ample opportunity for spiritual growth.

On my way home from work one day, I was offered a very unique perspective. There was a section of road where the traffic usually came to a standstill. Each day, I would use this time to meditate, that is, to be present and place the majority of my awareness in my body. But this particular day, I had an awakening. I became intensely present, as the traffic began to flow again. I was still able to sense the emotions of the drivers but this time, I perceived them in a whole new light.

Having given up all resistance, I allowed the emotions of the other commuters to flow through me. I received it all. I could sense aliveness and power in every single emotion. There was fear, anger, resistance and judgement flying in all directions but in my little car, there was only pure joy. I could sense each emotion and I recognised deeply that every such emotion was a manifestation of love. This sounds odd, I know. How can anger be love?

I understood that even the anger was an *asking* for love. These ugly manifestations were, in fact, a cry for love! How had I not seen this before? I had been judging my fellow humans, applying my filters and past experience and I had missed the whole point. They were all good people and they were simply wanting something better. At odds with the stress and chaos of it all, their emotions were crying out for something different, for release and for love. I knew that the power of my observation and the new perspective I offered helped some of the motorists, including myself, to heal. I felt like a supercharged Mario Kart character, as I blissfully glided my way home; amped up on the 'positive' vibes being offered. But this privileged perspective of mine was not to last.

My sense of bliss and joy came to pass after I fell asleep that night. This was to be yet another, short-lived awakening and I was dumped back into my regular state of neurosis thereafter, all the while trying my best to be 'normal.'

The next day, I found the commute to be particularly trying. Why was I feeling so frazzled? Was it the contrast compared with the day before? Everything seemed so hard-hitting. The traffic was so noisy and particularly frenzied. Where was the sense of bliss and peace that I'd had the day before?

I went through various stages of believing in a higher power over the years. On this particular day, since I was having such a difficult time coping, I asked for divine intervention. As I raged my way along in the mad rush of cars flying past like missiles, I awaited a sign or an awakening, *anything* to help me feel better! And just as I started doubting my request for help, writing it off as being 'silly,' I got my answer.

I didn't know what was going on at first, when the strange sound began. It was like a personified tea kettle being taken off the stove mid-squeal, warbling and whistling in fits and starts. The obstreperous sound became more insistent and bizarre when its source finally dawned on me. I laughed out loud; the simplicity of my plight was amusing. My window had been slightly ajar the whole time, causing the traffic to be especially noisy and upsetting to me. Soon after I asked for divine help, the answer came in the form of a breeze, forcing its way through the invisible crack. My window had never made such an absurd sound. I wound the window up fully and the car was peaceful. Thank you, universe, for comically highlighting such a simple solution.

Whenever I have asked for divine intervention, the answer is both simple and amusing. It's as if the universe is saying, 'Lighten up! Don't take life so seriously!'

There were a few insidious ideas that I picked up during my time at the ashram. This isn't the fault of the ashram, however. These ideas simply reflected some covert norms that crept in amongst the devotees. I believed I had to suffer my way to enlightenment, which was not achievable for me in this lifetime because I was not a designated 'master.' Now there's a fun belief to unravel! In my mind, I had to master all unpleasant situations in order to test myself and prove that I could be equanimous.

But life is about what you wish it to be about. You do not have to suffer to prove yourself or to become a master. Just be all that you are. If there is a better situation that you can move towards, you can do that! If winding your window up makes the drive quieter and offers more peace, you can do that!

It took me a long time to realise that life did not have to be about suffering. I simply chose some challenges early on, so that I would be forced to seek peace within, rather than relying on the material world for satisfaction. Once you have decided to go within, the world is your oyster! Really. When you be all that you are and when you embrace all that you are with joy and appreciation, you will find everything you need. And remember, the universe has a sense of humour. Remember to laugh often and lighten up, that is, let yourself be 'enlightened.' It's your true nature, after all.

Chapter 15

Meeting the Council

It was dark by the time I arrived, yet I was able to see the landscape beneath the starlit sky perfectly. I could feel the power of the majestic waterfall, as it cascaded over the amphitheatre-like cliff that wrapped around the large lake at its base. A lush green wildflower meadow carpeted the tiered rows that flowed out from the lake. I made my way up a stone staircase connecting to the top tier, where they awaited my arrival.

This meeting was special indeed. I felt great reverence as I approached. There were roughly twelve figures of imposing stature standing at the edge of the lake, with their attention fixed on me. They had been expecting me. I knew these beings were wise beyond measure; embodiments of the great mystery, the one consciousness. As I approached, they bowed, slowly and ceremoniously. I could not believe it! Here were these beings, wise and pure, bowing to *me*. This was at odds with my belief that one who is not a master does not deserve such high regard. I bowed in return but it didn't feel like the right thing to do. They, however, do not judge. My awkward feeling at having bowed was the result of my own judgment. It would have been better to receive their veneration.

These wise beings did not expect reciprocation. They know that we are one. As they offer their exaltation to me and as I graciously receive it, there is an inherent reciprocity.

It became clear to me in this moment that there is no such thing as hierarchy in the spiritual realms. I was seen clearly and honoured for all that I am. They do not withhold approval at one's transgressions, as a stern parent might. How can they when they see all that we are? Humans take on a huge task when they come to the earth. This place is challenging by its very nature. It is understandable that we will flounder at times, given all that we are dealt.

I was shown that in my 'smallness,' I am indeed an invaluable part of the whole. It is only the expectations that I place upon myself, that could ever take me away from awareness of their adoration.

You may not always feel that you live up to your honourable intentions in this life but you can never fail. If you could see yourself through their eyes, you would forgive absolutely any and all wrongdoings. You would not be so hard on yourself. There is nothing so terrible in this lifetime that would bring 'wrath' upon you from the non-physical realms. Only earthlings entertain such things.

When it is said that 'you can never get it wrong,' this is a reflection of the truth. Your life experience isn't dictated by a set of rules. You are free to choose within the confines of your human constructs.

You might question whether lack of accountability would result in barbaric behaviour, with humans descending into madness. In case you haven't noticed, humans are already descending into madness. The laws we have to govern human behaviour are not working. This is because, ashamed by our very nature, we try to suppress the shadows that well up from within. When you accept your shadows, however, they are held up to the light of consciousness and are transmuted. It is only that which you resist that grows stronger. You cannot suppress negative emotion for long. It will eventually explode in its calamitous glory.

There are consequences of resisting life. Resistance will simply take you away from the awareness of your true nature and connectedness with being. And that's okay; you are free to choose resistance or acceptance as life unfolds. Neither is right or wrong. You either move closer to, or away from, the love that you are.

Will awareness of the love available to you in this moment, trump the distractions offered to you in the form of a chaotic and tumultuous world? Will drama and challenges cease to lure you? Are you willing to give up complaint about how things are and accept each moment as a precious gift?

You have the free will to choose in each moment. You can never get it wrong and you have eternity. As you move away from the source; the light and love that you are, the return home is ever more joyous.

There was a belief that existed amongst many of the devotees at the ashram, that once we become fully awakened, we no longer reincarnate. Becoming awakened was made out to be the ultimate goal. The idea is, that if you fully awaken, you no longer have to be part of the cycle of birth and rebirth, as though it is such a terrible thing! Upon multiple glimpses of awakening, my affection for the earth and her inhabitants has grown. It is only in the unenlightened state; in the midst of suffering, that we would wish for annihilation.

You have eternity, from a spiritual perspective. When you are fully awakened, you will return simply for the joy of it. Life was not supposed to be about suffering but it is through suffering that we appreciate the light that we are.

Each individual life is a relatively small period of time compared with the vastness of our universe. There is only one of you. You will never be who you are again. If you are enjoying something, you do not wish for it to end. Imagine the way you eat your favourite delicacy. You savour it slowly, fully attending to each delicious mouthful. When you learn to embrace life, you will come back again and again.

This is what the council taught me. Life is to be savoured with reverence and deep appreciation. You are an aspect of divine perfection. You are adored beyond measure. You can never get it wrong. Revel in this life and celebrate all that you are!

Chapter 16

Ancient Wisdom

I am a coloniser on this land. My ancestors came from all over the globe and converged on this continent, culminating in me. Some of my closest family members are part of the mob here in Australia. Nevertheless, I inhabit stolen ground.

As a child, I didn't know that my stepfather was an indigenous Australian. He seemed to be derogatory towards black people. I couldn't understand his disrespectful nature towards a person due to the colour of their skin. You can imagine my surprise to learn that his mother was an aboriginal woman. I can only guess that my stepfather was trying to protect his interests by denying his culture. But this robbed his children, including my half-brother, of the opportunity to know great wisdom and cultural riches.

Many of my neurotic outbursts as a young woman involved trying to come to terms with the Western way of life. I was unable to fathom the harried nature of modern living and the way people seemed to be determined to get somewhere and 'make something' of themselves. This unchecked busy-ness and perpetual growth carries on even now, to the detriment of the very thing that sustains life; our natural environment.

The more time I spend in quiet contemplation, listening to country and observing her with alert curiosity, the more apparent it is that she is ingenious. This country is a complex jigsaw puzzle of interconnected mysteries and only the ancient ones and their descendants are privy to the intricacies of her workings.

Then came the colonisers. We commit the most abhorrent crimes not only against nature but against the people who have inhabited the land since time immemorial.

Does this make you angry? Do you feel guilty? Is your heart breaking? If this is so, it is important to let yourself feel what you feel. If you deny what you feel it will grow, unchecked, until it becomes obnoxious enough to get your attention. Embrace your feelings and allow them to be there. Assimilate them into your being. They are gifts but only when you accept them as such. It is important to accept things that cannot change. The past is one such thing. We cannot change our history but we can learn from it and move forward with grace.

When my mother was ill with cancer and making her transition, I was living in a tent on her property. This was during an exceptionally wet year. The extreme weather and flooding made life in a tent most unpleasant. One of my rock-climbing buddies had a property in a nearby town and offered his granny flat to me. He travelled a lot for work and was barely there, so it made sense for me to stay there in between visiting mum.

My friend had begun renovating the dilapidated old shack and it was coming along nicely. But there were older sections of the house that were creepy when I was there alone. I often felt as though I was being watched. If I acknowledged my feelings of being spied upon, I would get goosebumps and my hairs would stand on end. Each night that I slept out in the granny flat, I would wake up at precisely midnight, with the strong sense there were people in my room.

When my friend was home, I tentatively asked him about the feeling I'd had of someone watching me, expecting him to treat me like a crazy person. I asked him if he'd ever felt someone was there. He said he hadn't noticed anything. Of course, he hadn't! What was I thinking? But then he went on to tell me about the history of the home.

They Came to Wake Me

Out on the perimeter of the large backyard, bordering onto the fence, was an old barn. While I recall a few similar structures in the 1980s, it's rare to see these rickety old barns standing today. My friend told me that among other things, the barn was used to store flour. The local indigenous people had been stealing the flour, so the homeowners took matters into their own hands. They killed the people by poisoning the flour. I was heartbroken when my friend told me this story but it is relatively tame compared with other atrocities in our colonial history.

I have always found ownership of land to be an odd concept. I can understand that you may inherit a place to care for, in order to pass it on to future generations in perpetuity but ideally, you would be deemed worthy of such a task before having the honour to take it on. The colonisers commandeered a land that had been tended to with the utmost care for tens of thousands of years by its indigenous people. The colonisers were refusing to share the spoils of their farming practices. I think it reasonable to help yourself to resources available on a land to which you belong and from which you have been displaced.

I visit this and other sites of known massacres in meditation, to offer my condolences and my appreciation to the ancestors. I feel this is an excellent first step in the healing process. Like I said, we cannot change the events of the past but we can learn from them.

Many years later, I connected with some ancestors in the dream state. One night, I went to visit an old man in the desert, in Western New South Wales. I stood at the edge of a pit, that revealed fresh red earth. The old man instructed me to sit in the pit with my knees drawn up to my chest. Only my head was above the level of the ground. He then asked me to raise my head to the sky and open my mouth. As I did this, he pulled an invisible negative energy from my body, through my mouth. I was honoured to have received this healing session from him.

When I was house sitting for my aunty, I had four old women come to visit me in my sleep. My aunty's house is on the top of a hill overlooking the ocean. When the women came to take me to a ceremony, I knew I was in the presence of greatness. These women were wise elders, they were powerful and they were humble. I had the sense that I was like a remora in the presence of a great white shark. Only, there was no shame in being a remora, for even the humble little remora has its place in the manifested world. These women were majestic indeed. They possessed aeons of natural wisdom; they were intensely present and their hearts were open. The leader of the group is the only one who spoke. The others were silent as we made our way to a sacred site on the hill. I cannot consciously remember the ceremony thereafter but upon awakening, I felt different and something significant had shifted within me. I knew that tremendous healing had taken place.

I still cannot fathom why I have been the recipient of such generosity. I am deeply appreciative of the ancestors who inhabit the land to this day. I have since learned that the site of my aunty's house is near the burial place of a very important indigenous woman.

I am not at liberty to speak for the people who have inhabited this land since time immemorial beyond my direct experience. However, since I have been contacted by these old ones, I have had certain realisations and the messages are very similar. If we wish to continue as a species, we need to drastically change our ways. Each manifestation of earth is sacred and needs to be treated as such. To pick apart, dig up, flatten, bulldoze, cover with concrete, pollute and explode, are acts of grave insanity. I know that I am a hypocrite, as a modern human sitting here typing on my computer.

So, the message is simply this; go within and find contentedness. A content human does not perpetually consume. As we each awaken, we find the purity and simplicity of the present moment. From within the space of the now, 'right action' unfolds. We can hear the whispers of those who have gone before us and can be guided by their wisdom. Anything extraneous can be eliminated from life, which in turn, benefits the land.

If each of us were to contact the spaciousness within, we would see the world shift drastically in favour of the survival of our species. Small changes, towards caring for the planet, will go a long way towards ensuring our continuance. As you heal, you begin a new legacy and you just may create a new earth, upon which its multitude of species may thrive in all their splendour.

Chapter 17

Suspended In-Between

While my Life Between Lives regression was unsuccessful (see Alacqua), I have visited the 'in-between' on a number of occasions. The trouble is, it is difficult to convey with words.

When I was in my early twenties, I devoted all of my time (even my working hours) to my spiritual practice. I was reading 'The Power of Now' on repeat, as I enjoyed spending time in presence with the author, Eckhart Tolle. I devoured many spiritual texts at this time and was introduced to the concept of 'the space of no-mind.' Apparently, this was a space that one would enter during sleep. It is such an altered state of consciousness, relative to our waking state, that while each of us enters it, we do not recall it.

One morning, just prior to waking, I was having a silly dream about work. It was one of those dreams that is more akin to mind-babble; a regurgitation of the ordinary happenings of the day before. But things were about to get interesting. All of a sudden, I left my dream and expanded into great spaciousness.

There was stillness. Pure, all-encompassing stillness. I say 'there was stillness' and yet, the stillness was me and I was it. I was the all-pervasive silence. Suspended in eternity, I 'drifted' in pure expanded bliss. As I joyfully drifted in silence, I knew I was everywhere and everything and at the same time, I was nowhere and no-thing. This eternal and sacred moment was one of absolute rapture, an infinite moment of revelling in the 'sensation' of the creative intelligence, the joy that I am. This deeply satisfying place could be called 'home.' I knew, this is where I return to and the place from which I emerge. I could sense the perfection inherent in all.

There is an undeniable assuredness upon re-emergence into the space of no-mind. And indeed, the mind was still; there was no mind. Intelligence arose, knowing emerged as pure impressions, without the need for interpretation or language. Words merely reduce such purity to mental constructs. Words simply introduce confines that place an unfathomable intelligence into limiting little boxes. It is impossible to say how long I was in the space of no-mind. It felt like roughly eighty years or so but time has little bearing in such realms.

Time is the measurement of the movement of objects in space relative to one another. A day, is a full rotation of our planet. A year is the number of days or 'rotations' we complete as we orbit the sun. Each day is further divided into units of measurement that we call hours, minutes and so on. Given the incorporeal nature of 'objects' within the mysterious space of no-mind, time has little relevance there.

I left the spacious realm as suddenly as I had entered. I heard a static sound and I was plonked back into my silly little dream, excitedly chattering away to my work colleagues. 'Can you believe that!? I just entered the space of no-mind!' and on I prattled, my mind in overdrive, as if making up for the prior stillness with a vengeance.

My foolish chatter came to an instant halt when an authoritative 'boom' shook me out of my dream. Lightning had struck the aerial of my house. I sat in bed in stunned silence, contemplating the spaciousness. I marvelled at my fortune to consciously enter such a realm and recall it.

As you become aware of your oneness with consciousness, it is apparent that there isn't 'nothing.' There is a rich tapestry of both nothing and everything in a rapturous merging and separating of all that is and never was. The oneness, the intelligence that you are, is imbued with a love (for lack of a better word) that is deeply satisfying and joyful. You are that. It is only lack of awareness of the magnificence that you are that causes unrest in this lifetime.

This is the very thing that spiritual seekers are searching for. But you cannot search for what you are. You can only be that and be aware that you are that.

This life is a peculiar phenomenon; an expression of the one consciousness. You emerge and you re-emerge. The intelligence that imbues life is all-pervasive and is adoring of each form it takes. It celebrates the complexity and diversity of each individual experience. There is only one great tragedy in life; to spend your time searching for something you cannot lose. Again, there is but one reminder; be all that you are in this lifetime. Celebrate the form you have taken. Celebrate your uniqueness. You are adored beyond measure. The contribution you make to the evolution of consciousness is truly extraordinary and deeply appreciated. You are a sacred expression of the divine and the greatest mystery in the universe. That's pretty special, don't you think?

Chapter 18

My Angels Besse and Snot

When Snot arrived, she had no name. She was a boisterous young thing and took the whole family by storm. My stepdad was the self-appointed naming authority in my household, with tragic consequences. Snot was named based on the characteristic snoring noises that Staffordshire Bull Terriers make when they sleep.

She was my childhood angel. My household was a challenging place and I would often hide on the back step crying. Snot would poke her head up between my legs and lick my face. She was the sweetest pet and took excellent care of me.

When I was about three years old, some men were digging a large trench in my backyard with heavy machinery. Mum encouraged me to go out and see what they were doing. I stood at the edge of the trench, feeling tiny, as I peered down at the muddy earth. One of the men, who had been chatting with me, put his arm around me. I was extremely uncomfortable and Snot sensed this right away. She made it very clear that he was not to touch me, barking and snarling threateningly. He backed away and held his hands up in surrender. I felt quietly powerful.

If Snot wasn't being my guardian, she was up to mischief. If you've ever owned a Staffy, you'll know exactly what I mean!

On a weekend fishing trip, mum put a prawn on a hook and placed it down for a moment. When she turned back, the hook was missing and Snot was 'smiling' at her, wagging her tail, with fishing line protruding from her mouth. Snot ended up with a large scar down her side where the vet cut her open to remove the hook.

After mum moved on from that relationship, my stepdad gained custody of Snot. One day he called us with the tragic news she had gone missing and hadn't returned. It was impossible for her to have absconded of her own accord, given she was confined to a Staffy-proof fortress. Her enclosure had been carefully refined over the years after multiple escapes and litters of puppies. But she had always returned (pregnant) in the past, so it was very unlikely she had run away this time.

It looked like someone had broken into the yard and stolen her. What happened to Snot remained a mystery.

Many years later, Snot paid me a visit in a dream. I was in my childhood house and Snot came bursting in, full of life with her tail wagging itself into a hazardous stupor. The dream was pure, rambunctious enjoyment. I played with her for a time, fully immersed in her infectious delight. She seemed so puppy-like; I had to check that it was her by locating her scar from the prawn incident. The scar from her side was still there. This was indeed my beloved Snot. I knew then, that she had passed away. It was so nice to have closure and to see my childhood angel again.

I also had a furry angel at my dad's house. Besse was a scruffy and sweet terrier cross. She was never any trouble and loved to hang out with me, playing for hours on end. But as she got older, her quality of life declined. Dad would come home from work to find her lying in a ditch in the backyard, the poor dear. When he took her to the vet, she knew. She had her head on his leg staring at him the entire drive, which made it much harder for him.

Busy studying for my undergraduate degree, I was distracted from Besse's passing. I lived by myself in a small bedsitter. As a self-conscious young woman, I would weigh myself on my digital scales often. But they started malfunctioning. Whenever I stepped off the scales the digital display would flash (in square figures) 'bE55E'.

Trying to make sense of this weird red flashing, I would mumble things like 'Less 5?' thinking the scales were perhaps rudely tracking my progress. Then the 'bE55E' would disappear and a weight of either one or two kilograms would appear on the display before going blank.

This happened for quite a while and I became accustomed to my flamboyant scales, ceasing to question their bizarre behaviour.

One night, I had just finished watching a movie and was about to get ready for bed. I switched my VCR off and the display flashed 'GOODBYE' as usual and then flashed (in square figures) 'bE55E.' I sat there, dumbfounded for a moment, 'wasn't it my scales that were playing up?' I scratched my head, as I recalled the recent events. Yes, it had been the scales, I thought they were telling me to weigh less or something. Could this have been Besse reaching out to me all along? 'Besse?' I blurted out. 'Besse!' I repeated and sat for a while, remembering that lovable little friend of mine. Strangely, my household appliances ceased malfunctioning thereafter.

I'd had some strange spiritual happenings at that point in my life but I was very surprised that a pet could reach out to me in such a way. I had not considered the spelling of her name before but had I been given the chance to spell it, I would have opted for 'Bessie.' On every occasion that her name flashed on my appliances, it was spelled with a lower case 'b.' The digital display could have easily made an upper case 'b' with the number '8' so I found this both intriguing and adorable. Apparently, she spells her name 'besse.'

Humans can have a special bond with their pets. The beasts of the natural world are completely transparent to the light of consciousness. When we gaze into their sparkling eyes, we see the light of presence beaming back at us; the epitome of unconditional love. We are absolutely accepted and adored by our beloved pets. This connection can keep us sane in times of difficulty.

I've had many loved ones, including pets, pass away. It seems they often try to reach out to us, by multiple means, as if to say, 'I am alive. I am still with you. I am beaming with light and joy. I love you and all is well.'

Chapter 19

Big G

In high school English class, we were expected to keep a diary. When I read my diary retrospectively, I was blown away by some of the conclusions, in that they did not seem like the words of a teenage girl. It was as though they had not come from me but *through* me.

Channelling in writing is something I have done for a long time. When you read the work of a channel, it will often have a depth that resonates beyond the words. You will sense a powerful emanation of energy, that is deeper than the meaning of the words alone.

More recently I have been allowing myself to speak from a state of intense presence or 'beingness.' Beingness is our natural state, of which many humans are unaware due to a noisy mind. The states of bliss produced by beingness, feel easy and sustainable. It is simply allowing the mind to become still and being aware of the bliss that is your true nature. You have access to great wisdom and intelligence when you are intensely present.

Channelling, is opening to more energy than usual, allowing for a flow of great information and wisdom, like plugging into a network and 'downloading' the information. I distinguish 'being' from channelling in that when I channel, I can feel a great deal of energy flowing through me. It is like I am a lamp and instead of using a lower wattage globe, I have inserted one with a higher wattage, allowing more electricity to flow. Consequently, it feels as though channelling is not sustainable over a longer period of time. Being present, however, is sustainable.

I have also begun channelling through the spoken word. I hear channels being asked to share their experience when they are channelling and I was surprised with the striking similarities to my experience. There are some channels who, like me, have a difficult time keeping their eyes open. I am able to open my eyes with a bit of effort but when I do, all I can see is a white nebulous mist surrounding me, which intensifies as the energy does. It hurts my eyes if I try to see anything beyond the mist, so it's nicer to keep them closed.

Big G

In my twenties, I devoured the 'Conversations with God' series channelled by Neale Donald Walsch in utter fascination. How was it possible to write as if the answers were coming directly from God? As my channel opened, I realised that I too, could connect with something incontrovertibly wise within. We all have this ability. This is not a skill available to only a select few people. Each of us has access to higher wisdom.

About a year ago, inspired by 'Conversations with God,' I decided to have a go at writing to God myself. Why not? The only problem was that I have developed an aversion to the word 'God' due to its misuse by some people from my past. I decided to use the term, 'Big G' instead. This felt comfortable and familiar to me, as if I was speaking to a best friend. I became affectionately known as 'Little G' in the conversations that followed, although, this by no means represents hierarchy; just relative size.

Over the last year, the process of writing to and from Big G always brings me back to a state of balance if I am feeling out of sorts. If I am feeling good when I write, the process helps me to reach new heights of bliss.

To my surprise, even in the midst of emotional turmoil, I still receive sound advice and sober answers. The messages are always loving, often surprising and frequently humorous. God really does have a sense of humour.

Neale Donald Walsch understandably questions whether the conversations really were coming from God or just a wiser part of himself. I don't believe the question is pertinent. One of the reasons is that we don't really have a way of knowing the source of the information. We can only speculate. If, like me, you believe we are all a representation of the one consciousness, then essentially, it is like I am talking to me. You, me, God; we're ultimately one and the same. But throwing all of that aside, there is one final conclusion by which I measure these written works and it's this; does the source really matter? Is not the measure of the words in their effect on the reader? As in, if they have a healing, positive and unifying outcome, are they not then beautiful words to be considered, irrespective of their source?

If you would like to try this out for yourself, I highly recommend it. When you sit to write, imagine there is a wiser part of you that can speak through you. What does it say? Another helpful method, particularly if you are struggling with something, is to imagine talking with your future self, who has gained mastery over the situation. What advice does that future self give you? The words that follow may surprise you in their simplicity and power.

Big G

It is important to remember, you do not have to accept the advice that is given to you. You can choose to ignore it or come up with an alternative version that is more suitable. You will know if you are receiving advice from a wiser part of you because it will be uplifting, peaceful and loving, without exception. Any lower energies of fear or anger are not from source. Source will never coerce, manipulate or assert dominance over your free will.

I would like to share a very small excerpt from some of my conversations with you. I chose this excerpt because, one, I asked and the answer I received was to 'scroll' and two, the question is one that many people ask. Here goes!

Big G, what does life want from me?

Life wishes to be expressed *through* you. Be a portal for consciousness. You are awakening. Each moment you realise your tendency to gravitate towards complaint, negative emotions or the stream of thinking, you awaken. I am so proud of you. You are awakening, gravitating towards this moment, gravitating towards stillness more and more. Don't be so hard on yourself Little

G. You are awakening, just as you had always intended. You are right on schedule.

Big G, I would like more 'success' with life.

Be in your moments. Be ordinary. You *are* success. You are inseparable from that. Be all that you are in this moment. Life is moving *for* you in perfection. Even the lack of movement right now is *for* you and it is perfect, exactly as it was meant to be. You are noticing when the gravity of your emotions, your thoughts and so on, are attempting to draw you in. Simply keep noticing. Keep being present. Keep being all that you are.

I will. Thank you, Big G.

You're welcome. Truly. Always. I love you.

Chapter 20

What Does it all Mean?

Life is magical, exactly as it is. Indeed, there are mysterious occurrences that are termed 'supernatural' and seem extraordinary but the real magic is in the ordinary. The simple fact of life is a miracle in and of itself! Look at this planet and its complexities! Look at the biodiversity, the enchanting landscapes and evolutionary adaptations to a myriad of exotic environments. Even to this day we are discovering new species and learning of more ingenious adaptations. Life is undeniably imbued with wonder. It is just a matter of shifting perspective.

When the mind is cluttered and full of chatter, the sacredness of life is obscured. The mind analyses, labels, complains, comments and judges. As it does this, it reduces the world to mere concepts. The essence that pervades all things cannot be sensed and the world appears as dull and devoid of joy. This could not be further from the truth.

Jill Bolte Taylor expresses this poignantly in 'My Stroke of Insight' where she is drawn into euphoric assimilation with the state of oneness as a result of a haemorrhage occurring in the left hemisphere of her brain, temporarily disrupting the analytical mind. When this occurred, she immediately entered a state of surrender, aware of her oneness with all, expansive and in touch with a state of deep peace or 'Nirvana.'

Since her awakening occurred due to a physical phenomenon, an analytical mind could explain it away as 'Well, we would expect this from a brain disorder of this kind,' however, the experience has provided Jill with a greater sense of purpose and meaning.

While the left hemisphere of the brain is responsible for analytical and methodical thinking, this isn't a problem, unless we are unable to allow moments of silence and access to the right hemisphere. Ultimately, the ethereal cannot be fully grasped by the analytical mind. Jill encourages us to become more right-hemisphere-focused, so that humans may know the deep peace available to us in the here and now.

But the rest of us do not need to suffer strokes in order to witness the majesty of right hemisphere processing. We can simply focus on matters concerning the right hemisphere of the brain, such as the present moment. Meditation can provide an excellent aid for enabling the quieting of the analytical mind, allowing the kinaesthetic creativity of the right side of the brain to emerge. You do not have to abolish the analytical side of the brain altogether. It is undeniably useful and without it, we cannot function. The problem is that humans do not use the analytical mind; *it uses them.*

As for the extraordinary occurrences I have shared in this book, you do not have to seek them. They will become a part of your experience when and if necessary. The depths of peace available to you in each moment far surpass any supernatural experience.

I have shared these moments, as each contains within it a reminder to be open to the magic and wonder around us. The manifested universe is a mysterious place, to say the least but it is not to be feared. All other life forms are animated by the one life, the one consciousness. The events that occur are always in our favour, if only we can see them as such and move with the flow of life, it can work for us.

The intelligence that creates worlds also moves in you. It can never abandon you, for you are it. It is only a human mind that is incapable of being still for a moment, that can distract you the magnificence that you are.

I have given up questioning the reality of these events long ago. To me, there is no point in understanding whether the occurrences shared in this book really happened. The memories are more vivid than many of my physical earthly experiences so, in some ways, they are more real. But reality is a highly subjective matter.

I only measure each experience by this; 'Ye shall know them by their fruits.' These events have brought about healing, along with greater love and appreciation for the manifested world. I feel blessed to have been privy to such wonders. That is some delicious and nourishing fruit.

A few years ago, I went to visit a life coach and he offered me an affirmation; 'I don't know what this or anything else means.' As I used this affirmation, its purpose became clear. It can help keep the mind from jumping to conclusions. I know that as I enter the present moment deeply, if answers are required, they will arrive.

It is good to be comfortable with not knowing. We do not have to analyse and solve every single mystery in the universe. Do we really want to live in a world without mystery?

It is a joy to be able to observe the earth with the clarity of presence, relieved of the veil of past perceptions that can distort our view.

But don't make the state of presence, that is, enlightenment into a goal. Having goals can contribute to a fulfilling existence but enlightenment *is* your nature. By placing something that you *already are* into the future, your awareness of it will perpetually elude you. You don't awaken in the future; you awaken now. It is because you are awakening to the magic and wonder all around you that this book has called to you. This is you becoming aware of who you are and being privy to the truth of your nature.

As you go about your day, see if you can sense the aliveness inherent in all things. Even the seemingly inanimate contains a certain aliveness. Be aware of the energy that animates your form. Do this now. And now. And now. Each time you notice the mind has taken you over, the light of consciousness grows within you.

We look for awakening as though we are looking for something extraordinary but there is nothing extraordinary in it. We seek the grand achievement of enlightenment and think 'Oh, no, that can't be it, it's too ordinary. It must be elsewhere.' And on it goes, looking somewhere else, continuously seeking this extraordinary thing.

That is why there is no need to make it into a goal. Just be all that you are now. If there is discomfort now, embrace it. It will pass. But don't try to be rid of it. Your moments present to you as they will. So, begin where you are now. Stay with it. Sense the aliveness of your being and realise deeply that you are extraordinary; you are a miracle, in this moment, exactly as you are.

If I were to say that I understand the mysteries of the universe, it would ultimately rob me of the enchantment I have witnessed. It is clear that there is an interconnectedness of all things. There are connections of the one life on an unfathomable scale. When you look out at the night sky, what do you see? Forms upon forms, mysterious worlds brimming with light, juxtaposed with the stupendousness of empty space. We scarcely know what is here on the earth, let alone out there in the solar system, the galaxy and countless other galaxies. The known universe is indeed mystifying and miraculous.

It all seems so real, doesn't it? I suspect, when we pass from this earth we will rejoice and most likely laugh! We will marvel at how seriously we took ourselves and how precious we were about certain little things, that no longer matter. It will all seem so trivial and so simple. Why didn't we laugh more, play more and celebrate the miracle that is our existence!? Why did we remain stubbornly stuck on suffering? Why not choose to shift towards the light and joyous experiences of life? Why weren't we more unashamedly loving and kind towards others?

When we pass from this earth, we will view the great mystery and experience deep reverence and appreciation, so all-consuming and pure, that words fail to describe it. You will celebrate the life that you are and you will be eager for more. But why wait? Why not know yourself as that right now? For you are inseparable from that; you are the greatest mystery in the universe and that is indeed worth celebrating.

About the Author

Rachel Blacker is a spiritual teacher and emerging author born in Western Sydney, Australia. Rachel describes her upbringing as 'tumultuous' and 'a smorgasbord of emotions'. Motivated by her challenging childhood, she went on to complete a science degree. During this time, a move to the mountains ignited her passion for the natural environment. When Rachel began working for a large company in her field of expertise, she came to realise that she was not feeling joy in her life and that something had to change.

She decided to embrace her meditation and yoga practice and make changes in her life that were more in alignment with her true values. She sought employment that enabled her to spend more time connecting with nature and the outdoors. Her time spent in the mountains helped to hasten her spiritual awakening and she found comfort in the warm embrace of Mother Nature.

The untimely death of her mother further cemented Rachel's decision to seek meaning beyond the daily grind of full-time work and prompted a move to the coast. Rachel had always felt a pull towards the ocean and in 2011, she moved to the scenic north coast of New South Wales and took up surfing. She hasn't looked back. For Rachel, spending time in nature and in the ocean has been key to her spiritual wellbeing. During her time on the coast, she met her soul mate, Charlie. Together, they have embraced their ideal life, following their intuition at every step. They have spent the last seven years travelling together in their beautiful self-built camper van between Charlie's hometown in South Australia and Rachel's adopted home in Northern New South Wales.

Rachel has continued to work on her passions and has completed training in meditation, neuro-linguistic programming, hypnosis and life coaching. Rachel and Charlie continue to work together on their projects, which they hope will improve spiritual wellbeing and appreciation of nature in Western society.

Recommended Resources

Hot Chocolate for the Mystical Soul: 101 True Stories of Miracles, Angels and Healing by Arielle Ford (Thorsons, 1998)

The Power of Now: A Guide to Spiritual Enlightenment by Eckhart Tolle (New World Library, 1999)

Living with Joy: Keys to Personal Power & Spiritual Transformation by Sanaya Roman (HJ Kramer Inc. Publishers, 1986)

Conversations with God: An Uncommon Dialogue by Neale Donald Walsch (Hachette Australia, 1996)

The Law of Attraction: The Basics of the Teachings of Abraham by Esther Hicks & Jerry Hicks (Hay House, 2007)

My Stroke of Insight: A Brain Scientist's Personal Journey by Jill Bolte Taylor (Penguin Books (1 May 2009)

Destiny of Souls: New Case Studies of Life Between Lives by Michael Newton (Llewellyn Worldwide Ltd; 1st edition (30 June 2000)

Also by Rachel Blacker

Finding the One- A Practical Guide to Manifesting Your Soul Mate

In *Finding the One* Rachel guides you on a process that will help you fall in love with life, fall in love with yourself, find completeness within and magnetise the romance of a lifetime. Using inspirational stories as examples, Rachel breaks down the barriers of cultural conditioning and applies compelling spiritual teachings that will lead you on a path to joyful living and powerful manifestation.

Finding the One- Soul Mate Manifestation Workbook

Finding the One- Soul Mate Manifestation Workbook contains beautiful processes with prompts, to bring your desire for your soul mate relationship to life. It helps you highlight that which may be standing in your way, enabling you to move towards the relationship of your dreams. When you feel complete and deeply satisfied; when you match the vibration of your desire, your soul mate must find you.

www.ingramcontent.com/pod-product-compliance
Lightning Source LLC
Chambersburg PA
CBHW011150290426
44109CB00025B/2562